Chapters In The Life Of Elsie Ellis...

Hetty Bowman

ELSIE ELLIS.   *Frontispiece.*

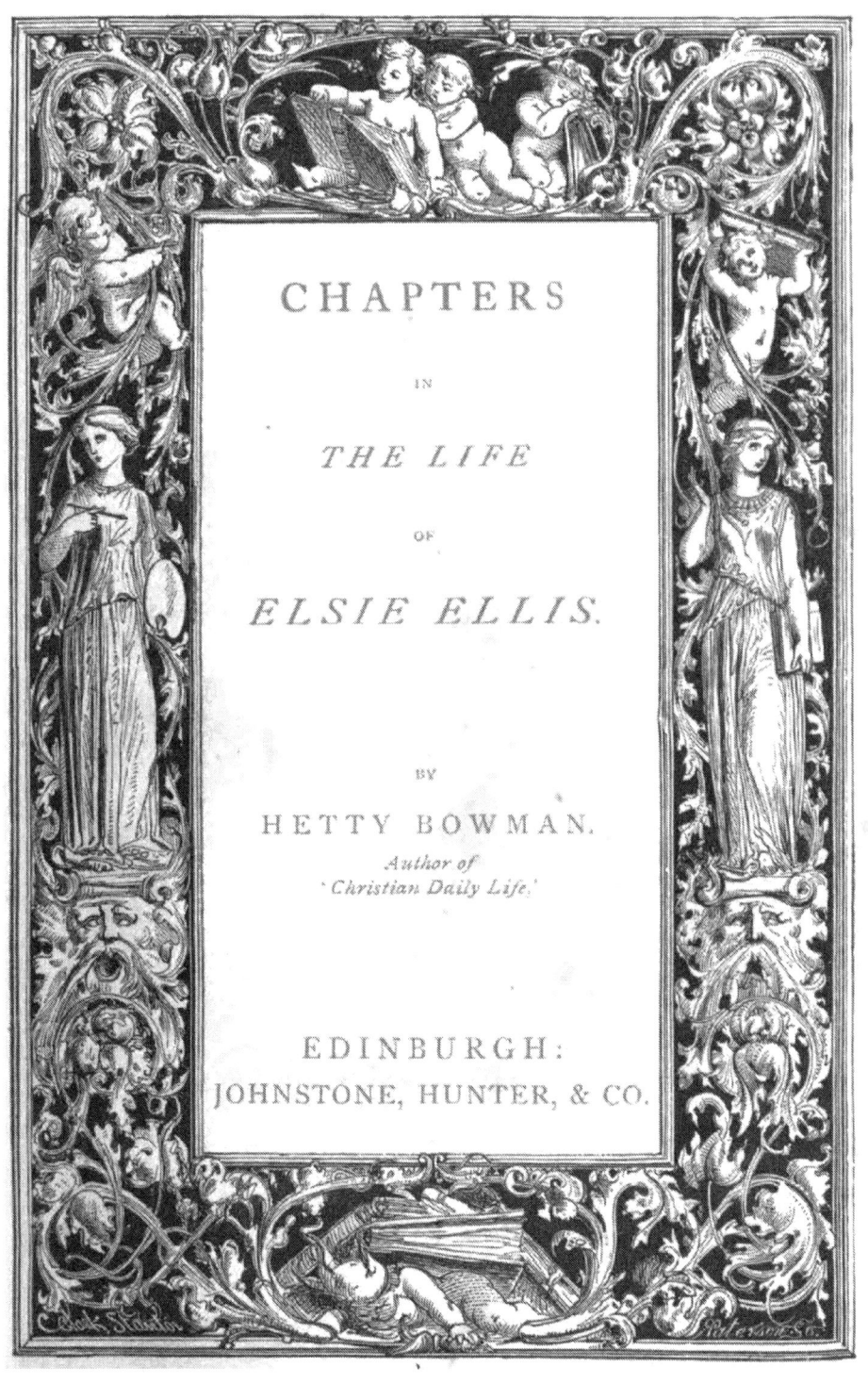

CHAPTERS

IN

THE LIFE

OF

ELSIE ELLIS.

BY

HETTY BOWMAN.

Author of
'Christian Daily Life.'

EDINBURGH:
JOHNSTONE, HUNTER, & CO.

Crawford & M'Cabe, Printers, 15 Queen Street, Edinburgh.

I.

A LITTLE CHILD IN THE OLD HOUSE.

'O how I long to travel back,
  And tread again that ancient track !
  That I might once more reach that plaine
  Where first I left my glorious traine,
  From whence the enlightened spirit sees
  That shady City of Palm-trees.'

HENRY VAUGHAN.

A

ELSIE ELLIS.

CHAPTER I.

A LITTLE CHILD IN THE OLD HOUSE.

 AM an old woman now,—at least I am
sure I ought to be, with all these children
growing up about me. Bless them! the
darlings, with their wistful, wondering eyes,
in which I love to watch the new thoughts
gleaming one by one; and their curious,
incomprehensible speeches, that seem to me always like
mysterious fragments of some forgotten lore.

However, I mean to write about myself, not about
the children. But you see I have begun to ramble
already, like an old woman as I am; so I fear there
will be many digressions and parentheses in this history.

Yet, after all, I am not so very old. People seem quite young at sixty now-a-days, and only moderately middle-aged at three-score and ten. But when I was young, even forty years appeared a venerable antiquity, and I have certainly overstepped that boundary.

I am going to write the story of my life. Not but that it has been a very ordinary one—the early part of it especially so, differing little in outward circumstance from that of thousands of English girls who grow up to womanhood in the sheltered homes of our middle classes. But precisely for this reason I will write it; for the world is so full of extraordinary things and persons, that I think the life of a commonplace woman may be a refreshing variety, and if no one cares for it, it will amuse the children by and by. Even now, I do not find that any fairy tales are half so interesting to them, as stories out of the wonderful old time 'when mamma was a little girl.'

I think I see it yet—the quaint, brown parsonage, with its low roof and deep window-seats, which was my childhood's home. In later years I found out that the old house was as inconvenient as it was picturesque; but that mattered little in the days when all this material world was still an enchanted palace, full of mystery and delight. Full, too, of manifold fears, vague and terrible; for one of my earliest recollections is of lying awake one stormy winter's night, listening to the wild moaning of the wind among the trees, and the rattle of panes in the leaden window-frames, till I held my very breath for fright, and felt firmly persuaded that an ' earthquake was going to be,' as I wrote next morning in large text hand, in a blank copy-book, which held the record of anything that seemed to my small mind worthy of being thus chronicled.

But I did not write, what has remained engraved on memory's tablets ever since, in characters never to fade —that when my fear had almost reached a climax, and would certainly the next moment have ended in a scream, my mother entered the room with a light, and soothed me with gentle word and touch, and told me of Him who rules the storm, and who would surely care for His little trembling child. And then she knelt by my bedside, and repeated, 'Our Father, which art in heaven,' and the collect, 'Lighten our darkness.'

Ah! many a time since then, when the storms of life have been wild and high, and my faithless heart full of sad forebodings, I have thought how sweet it was to look up through the darkness and feel my Father near, with the promise which that childish memory clothes with deeper tenderness, 'As one whom his mother comforteth, so will I comfort you.'

I do not remember much of my mother; but this and one or two other mental photographs always rise clear and fair before me when I think of her. She died when I was not quite seven years old, leaving my brother Ernest and me to the care of her youngest sister, who was thenceforth to be my father's house-keeper. Ernest was my senior by six years; so I had not much companionship from him, especially as, soon after my mother's death, he was sent to a school at some distance. So I grew up a solitary little maiden, with many strange thoughts and fancies in my brain, which were rehearsed only to Carlo, the large New-foundland, which was my daily playfellow and protector.

I think I must have been a particularly naughty child, at least I have a clear recollection of several tremendous outbursts of passion, which were succeeded by fits of penitence as deep as they were transient. These tempests called forth grave rebuke, and still more grave chastisement from my good aunt, whose much-enduring spirit I now see that I must have sorely tried. At times she was obliged to hand me over to my dear father, who used to take me into his study, and lecture me upon my shortcomings and the general wickedness of my ways, until I was much impressed by the solemnity of the occasion, and might, perhaps, have been permanently benefited; only that, when I began to cry, he never could help kissing and comforting me, a proceeding which greatly marred the effect of his admonitions.

As to my education, it was conducted in a manner which would now be thought extremely unorthodox; but, on looking back, I cannot but think it was much more healthful and judicious than the present high pressure system, by which young minds are over-loaded, and young brains over-worked. Indeed, I have often congratulated myself that my 'teens' were completed before the machinery of education became so extremely complicated and oppressive. An hour's steady work in the schoolroom morning and afternoon (it *was* work, however, calling out all my powers, and keeping them at full stretch), this was all till the Rubicon of twelve was passed, which my kind preceptor required.

I was further obliged to devote a certain time daily to certain mysterious operations with the needle, wherein dear Aunt Margaret's patience and my own temper were often strained to their utmost limit.

But I am not aware that these demanded any special mental exertion, and the rest of the day was at my own disposal. Bright, happy hours! when play was real play, innocent of any attempt to combine amusement with instruction; when I gathered flowers because I loved them, not because I was required to arrange them in classes; when I fed caterpillars, yclept 'woolly bears,' because I loved them too, and not because they belonged to any particular genus or species.

How pleasant were the rambles in field and lane, or over the bright, breezy moorland, gathering unconscious knowledge of nature and her many wonders; laying up in memory's storehouse pictures, always flooded with sunshine, which have quieted my spirit many a time and oft, when it was fretted by the strife and dust of daily cares; above all, gaining health, that priceless gift, which is so often sacrificed to the excessive demands of modern education!

I believe that in other respects also I was no loser, for it seems to me that children sometimes learn more by being taught less. They extemporize for themselves a sort of instruction, which, although somewhat desultory, is still of good service. Energies not exhausted in the school-room will find free play out of it. Intellectual hunger will satisfy itself, and may very safely be left to do so with the food most congenial to its taste, provided only that a strict watch is kept, lest it should seize upon any unwholesome nutriment.

For myself, I am sure that not the least important part of my education was carried on in an old apple tree, where, in the delicious summer afternoons, I perched myself in a convenient angle, with the chosen volumes of history, poetry, or biography, which were read and re-read until they became a part of my very life. How curiously the light fell upon the page through the leafy screen above me, and how the orchard grass beneath was 'counter-changed with dusk and bright,' as the soft air crept through the branches! I could not, at this time, glance over those well-conned pages, without feeling on my cheek a sweet breath from the dear old days gone by.

Is it not true that our first books have some of the freshness and glow of our first friendships? There were certain numbers of the *Saturday Magazine*, a periodical which long ago finished an honourable career, that I shall ever hold in grateful remembrance. Its pages supplied a wonderful amount of information about birds, and flowers, and insects, which could hardly have been gained so pleasantly from elementary treatises on botany and entomology. Indeed, I am not sure that this same chosen friend and counsellor did not suggest the daring idea of a certain chemical experiment, which ended, it is needless to remark, in ignominious failure.

And was not all this education? Was it not mental wealth, all the more precious, all the more real, because I was wisely left to dig it for myself, from mines of my own choosing? There were many difficulties in my way —so much the better for me; for is not that which we earn ourselves with pains and toil, a greater gain than many a gift?

None of my lessons gave me much trouble, except arithmetic, over which more tears were shed than I care to recall even now. Grammar also I did not greatly affect; but this I maintain to have been Lindley Murray's fault, not mine, for he has certainly succeeded in placing the noble science before 'the mind of youth,' as he himself would say, in as unattractive a form as could well be devised. My only consolation in his dry pages was to be found in studying the examples of versification at the end, and pondering, curiously, what kind of creatures dactyls and spondees might be, and how many 'feet' they had! One of his rules also occasioned me much grave speculation : 'Two negatives in English destroy one another,' etc. It always suggested to me a vision of two horned creatures engaged in deadly combat, and was invariably associated in my mind with a picture of the lion and the unicorn

'Fighting for the crown,'

which hung over the chancel of our village Church.

But I must not linger over these reminiscences, which may not be so interesting to my readers as to myself. Yet I cannot think them entirely idle ; for I suppose a vivid remembrance, of our own past, will be our best guide in exploring the mysterious child-nature, which we sometimes treat so awkwardly and ignorantly; and, perhaps, if our recollections were more accurate, and more carefully consulted, we should be saved from some mistakes in handling an instrument, whose delicacy we hardly realize until we discover, too late, that a careless touch has put it out of tune for ever.

II.

A PEEP INTO THE WIDE WORLD.

'Nay, I will turn the pages
  To where the tale is told,
Of how a dawn diviner
  Flushed the dark clouds with gold.

'And see, that ligh t has gilded
  The story, nor shall set ;
And, though in mist and shadow,
  You know I see it yet.'

A. A. PROCTOR.

CHAPTER II.

A PEEP INTO THE WIDE WORLD.

T just occurs to me that I have never stated either my name or place of abode—assuming, as we are all apt to do, that what is familiar to myself must needs be so to others. My dear father was the Rev. John Ellis, incumbent of Heatherstone, a small parish in the west of Cumberland. I grew up under the shadow of the hills, and the mountain streams, with their flashes of sunshine and depths of cool shadow, were my playmates, always fresh and pure, and ready with a responsive echo to the mood of the moment.

Our little village was very quiet and quaint— remote even yet 'from the railway and the steamboat, and the thoughts which vex mankind,'—and in those days almost entirely secluded, having its pulses stirred but rarely by tidings from the busy world without. The

Church and parsonage stood on opposite sides of the triangular plot of ground, called by courtesy a 'green,' the possession of which was constantly disputed by geese, and donkeys, and troops of yellow-haired children ; so that any enterprising blades of grass which had the hardihood to appear, were in danger of summary extirpation.

The Church—well, I had better not shock you by attempting to describe it. It could boast of purity in its ugliness, however, and was throughout in perfect keeping with itself—guiltless of all attempts at inharmonious decoration. To me there was something solemn in this very simplicity; and though I can never think that God is honoured by the poverty of His temple, I have realized the shadow of His presence there, as I have often failed to do in buildings of higher pretension. But this is perhaps a matter of early association. My father's voice proclaimed from that rude pulpit the way of life and peace, and through the half-open door I could watch the sunbeams falling tenderly upon my mother's grave.

When I was about twelve years old, the first break occurred in the still current of my life. How well I remember the shock of that overwhelming announcement that I was to be sent to school! Aunt Margaret told me of it one bright evening in spring when I had come in tired of play, and had thrown myself on a stool at her feet, as I generally did, to be kissed and petted before I went to bed. In what form she conveyed the sad news I do not precisely remember; but I know that, after she had explained to me, with much force of reasoning, the necessity for learning many things which neither she nor my father could teach, and set forth in glowing colours the charms of school-life, her eloquence suddenly failed, and she took me in her arms, and cried as if her heart would break. Dear, dear Auntie! never had child a tenderer second mother.

My pillow that night was wet with many tears. Children's trials are very real, in spite of all the pains and wisdom which we sage elders spend in proving the contrary. And so, when the day of parting really came, and I drove off with my father in the 'light cart' which was to convey us to the point where we should meet the Carlisle coach, and lost sight of my dear old home, with Aunt Margaret standing at the gate, and Carlo, poor fellow, watching us with a look of real sorrow in his honest eyes, and Betty waving a towel from the kitchen window by way of a farewell salute, I thought my little heart was so full of sorrow that it must certainly break. Poor small maiden! It was my first taste of parting, and very bitter I found it.

We did not reach our destination until the evening of the following day, for a coach journey succeeded to the 'light cart,' and, for convenience, we remained a night in Carlisle. What a strange new world it was to me, this my first glimpse of a town with any pretensions to size! I remember sitting at the hotel window, gazing out into the busy street, feeling already many years older, and gleaning wonderful items of information to be retailed to Betty and Carlo in the holidays! But the tears *would* gather and fall again whenever I thought of home; and my father, catching sight of the troubled little face, dismissed me to bed under care of the chamber-maid, wisely judging that I should forget my sorrows in sleep, as, in our blessed childhood, we are privileged to do.

The next day, when we had nearly reached our journey's end (which, by the way, was a market town in the county of Durham), my father suddenly said to me—

'Elsie' (this was my name, reader—short and quaint enough), 'do you know that Mary Wilton is to be your companion at school?'

I said 'No,' and thereafter fell into a long fit of musing upon this piece of intelligence, which was certainly anything but pleasant to me. Mary Wilton was the eldest daughter of our family doctor, who lived in a small country town about six miles from us. I had never seen her; but from my very babyhood she had been held up to me as a model of all the virtues which were so signally wanting in myself. I do not quite know how this came to pass, but so it was ; and, as the most natural of all consequences, out of very perversity I disliked her cordially, and privately made up my mind that, upon no possible consideration, should she ever be admitted to the honour of my friendship,—a resolution which I now emphatically renewed, closing my lips upon it with all due decision. How little I guessed the life-long blessing against which I was thus contradictiously locking up my heart! How little I knew the wealth of love and joy it would bring with it! But I am anticipating.

School-life was very happy, in spite of my gloomy forebodings. The yearning for home and home-love was at first very strong; but, as this gradually wore off, I took kindly root in the new soil. Yet, for many weeks I never slept without weeping, or woke without a dreary feeling of loneliness, which made me sick at heart. Sundays were the happiest days, for the familiar words of our Liturgy were a link to distant dear ones, and the house of prayer seemed a bright meeting-place, where, for a brief season, we were together before 'Our Father.'

> ' And surely, in a world like this,
> So rife with woe, so scant with bliss,
> Where fondest hopes are oftenest cross'd,
> And fondest hearts are severed most,
> 'Tis something that we kneel and pray
> With loved ones near and far away—
> One Lord, one faith, one hope, one care,
> One form of words, one hour of prayer.'

Retford Church was an Abbey, one of the noble piles into which our fathers built their hearts, enshrining them in stone, as a legacy for the future—a legacy, as Ruskin says, 'of even more than their hearts' blood, for it is of

P

their souls' travail.' And arch, and pillar, and fretted roof awoke a new sense within me, and I held deep communings with the mysterious past, and heard its voice, and felt its touch upon my soul.

And in Retford Church, kneeling side by side with Mary Wilton, I was confirmed. There was not much preparation in those days for that solemn rite ; but my dear father's letters supplied the lack of other teaching, and it was to me, as I believe it is to many, a time of much earnest feeling. I began to think seriously of many things which had hitherto been taken for granted ; and though this breaking up of childhood's unconscious trust is in itself rather loss than gain, it was in my case mercifully made the preparation for lessons of still deeper faith—faith often hardly won, through conflict, and doubt, and darkness, yet in turn strengthened even by these. The Great Teacher himself drew near to me, in my blindness and ignorance ; and though at first I did not know His voice, and would not regard it, He led me gently on, through many humbling discoveries of weakness and sin, till He brought me to rest at His feet, feeling, as a bitter reality of my personal consciousness, that there was 'no health in me,' but receiving from Him, the one Physician and Saviour, the touch of healing and the breath of life.

Oh! how thankful I have often felt that I gained, thus early, the shelter of 'the Rock!' In the centre of my being, peace for the most part reigned henceforth ;

but peace did not yet spread over its whole extent, more especially did not reach that part of it which came under the influence of things external. Many a lesson I had yet to learn in the school in which God trains His children; and as this spiritual discipline is often wrought through outward circumstances, I cannot doubt that it was the unseen Teacher's hand which laid before me some pages in life's history, which were a little hard to read, and blotted by fast-falling tears.

I do not intend to give here the history of my school days, which glided over, dark and bright, until I was seventeen, when my father told me I might continue my studies at home, and add some others not included in Miss Tracy's prospectus. I took leave of my kind governess with real regret; but among the girls I had made only one friend. Any penetrating reader can guess whom—Mary Wilton. Although her character seemed to lie at exactly the opposite pole to my own, I was drawn to her by a perverse sort of attraction, which I could neither explain nor resist. Perhaps there was a dash of contradiction in it after all, for she was hardly a favourite with the rest of our little group, though no one could say that she was ill-tempered or disobliging. But there was something in her calm, cold manner which made every one fall back, and leave her in the isolated position she seemed to prefer. Wherefore I, in my wilfulness and perversity, determined to attack the citadel forthwith, which I did, and

carried it, whether by force or stratagem I cannot say.
But I was astonished at my own success, and still more
astonished when I gradually discovered the riches which
lay behind that somewhat unpromising exterior.

Still I was often sorely puzzled about her. It would
have been hard to say, perhaps, that anything in Mary's
character was not what one liked, and yet there was a
want in it which I *felt*, though I could not define.
Perhaps it was not a want after all, but rather an excess
of qualities in themselves excellent. It seemed as if no
one was necessary to her—as if her nature was self-
contained and self-supporting, asking no sympathy from
others, and bestowing little upon them—little, that is, in
the true sense, for to sympathize indeed, we must give
forth more of ourselves, than at that time seemed
possible to Mary Wilton. Was this, again, merely
manner? Was it but another fold of a complex character, beneath the outer one of courtesy and grace, but
not her real self after all? Was this still far behind?
Was she like some mysterious cipher, never to be read
till some unthought-of key, perhaps a great sorrow,
revealed its true significance? I could not tell. I could
only wait and hope.

For myself, I do not think my character contains
any intricate nooks and corners. What there is in it,
lies on the surface, and anything which cannot be found
there need never be sought below it. In appearance,
Mary and I were as strongly contrasted as in mind.

'Night' and 'Morning,' we used to be called at school, for she was fair and slight, with grey eyes and rich auburn curls; while I inherited from my mother, who was Irish, the dusky hair and dark blue eyes which told of Milesian blood. Edward used to call my eyes violet before we were married. I do not remember that he has ever done so since.

III.

CHANGES.

'The thoughts of youth are long, long thoughts.'

LONGFELLOW.

CHAPTER III.

CHANGES.

HOW well I remember the evening of my return home, when, at length, school-life was over! I was a little disappointed that my father did not meet me at the inn where the coach stopped; but there was the well-known 'light cart,' driven by an honest farmer from the village, who took especial care of me and my property, and seemed to feel great satisfaction that I was coming back to Heatherstone 'to bide,' as he expressed it.

There were many thoughts in my mind, as we drove rapidly through the still air. The hills were purple in the sunset light; the long, bright day was dying slowly over the western sea, and the evening incense of fragrance rose softly from fields and flowers. I could have fancied that the trees waved their long arms over me in loving welcome, and the rooks cawed a drowsy greeting, as they wheeled in lazy circles overhead. For I was still—

> 'Standing with reluctant feet
> Where the brook and river meet,
> Womanhood and childhood fleet.'

The untrodden ground before me looked very fair in its promise, and in the ringing voices which seemed to call me onward, there were no undertones of grief.

But our drive came to an end, and my musings with it. There, at the gate, stood my father, and Carlo, and Ernest, home for a short holiday from the solicitor's office in which he was now articled. But no aunt Margaret, who had always been the first to welcome me. Where could she be? My companion, to whom I addressed this question, remarked oracularly, with an odd smile lurking in the corners of his mouth, that 'he supposed she would have other fish to fry;' whereat I wondered greatly.

'Welcome home, my darling!' were my father's first words; and then he led me hastily into the house, hardly leaving me time to snatch a kiss from Ernest, and bestow a passing pat on Carlo, whose great paws were on my shoulder in rather overwhelming welcome. And when I asked for aunt Margaret, the dear good man gave me no answer, till he had drawn me into his study, and shut the door, when he struck me dumb by the announcement that she was to be married the next day!

My first impulse was to be very indignant. 'Why

was I not told of this before?' I asked, in a tone of injured pride.

'Your aunt did not wish it,' replied my father; 'and I did not care to damp your pleasure in the prospect of coming home. I hope you will not be very lonely, darling,' he added, drawing me fondly to him; 'you must be my companion and housekeeper now; and we will have many happy days together, I trust, if God will.'

My darling father! Yes, there could be no doubt of that; but my ideas were in a state of uncomfortable confusion, and I listened almost without comprehension, while he went on to explain that aunt Margaret had been engaged for many years, in fact, before my mother's death, to a gentleman of some property in one of the southern counties; but that she would not consent to be married till she had first filled a mother's place to her dead sister's children, and seen me grown to woman's estate. All which my reason acknowledged to be very noble and self-denying; but still I would hardly accept it in expiation of the present offence.

'Why need aunt Margaret trouble herself to get married?' I wondered. And this man: he couldn't love her very much, or he wouldn't have waited eighteen years without once coming to see her! Of course I had no right to be angry. If she choose to marry the 'Autocrat of all the Russias,' it could be no concern of mine. But I *was* angry, nevertheless, whether with or without reason, I stayed not to inquire.

'What sort of a person is he, this Mr—?'

'Mr Merton. You must see him, my dear, and judge for yourself. But remember, that your aunt is a woman of sense and judgment, and her choice must be respected.'

My father coughed rather drily, I thought, and I immediately concluded that his own opinion was not favourable. Women of sense,—ay, and men of sense too, do unaccountable things, sometimes, in this same matter of matrimony.

But there was no opportunity for further questioning, for the door opened quietly, and aunt Margaret herself came in, looking rather shy, almost timid, but very happy withal, and with a light in her kindly eyes which I had never seen there before. I kissed her, rather ungraciously, I fear, and then said I would go to my room and take off my bonnet. A new dress was lying on the bed, in which I supposed I was to officiate as bridesmaid on the morrow; but I threw it aside impatiently, feeling much inclined to roll it up in a bundle, and crush it to its death. For, you perceive, I was no heroine, reader, but only a very wilful girl, with strong passions, as yet sadly undisciplined.

But, in time, gentler thoughts came over me, and, reflecting philosophically that it is never wise to make a trouble of what cannot be helped, I dressed as quickly as possible, went downstairs, and was introduced to Mr Merton.

The first impression was unpleasing; and though I reasoned against it as premature and prejudiced, I could not bring myself to believe that those thin lips, with their cynical corners, and those light blue eyes, cold and clear as a frosty sky, boded any good for poor aunt Margaret's future. I believe we took one another's measure at the first glance, and knew, by subtle but sure intuition, that, however outwardly courteous, we should always be alien, if not antagonist.

The evening passed, and so did the next morning, with its curious mingling of many feelings, and we watched the 'happy pair' drive off, amidst a shower of slippers which Ernest had, with great pains and diligence, collected for the occasion. He also bade us adieu the same evening, and my father and I were left to our solitude.

And a very pleasant solitude it was. My time was so fully occupied with books and work, and in visiting the schools and the poor, that I had no leisure to feel lonely. My dear father gave me plenty of mental employment. He was of opinion, that the training in classical lore, which was good for boys, must be equally beneficial to girls; so he made me return to the Latin exercises which my school-life had interrupted, and in time led me on to the yet nobler Greek. Many happy hours we passed together,—

> ' While a girlish voice was reading,
> Somewhat low for ai's and oi's.'

I think my father was right; for though there may be small place or need in a woman's life for classical knowledge, the mental discipline of such a course of study is, beyond doubt, bracing and healthful. And inasmuch as in 'all labour there is profit,'—provided only that it is consecrated by a loving look upward,— I believe that for every acquirement God will find a place in His plan of our life; and that every seed of knowledge cast into the mind's soil will one day spring up, either to bless another or to make the 'solitary place glad.'

However, there were other studies, not strictly classical, which might have justly claimed some share of my attention. The benefit of degree examinations for women may be always an open question; but there can be no doubt of their need of training in the routine of domestic management. Not that the one need ever clash with the other; for there is not the smallest foundation for the idea, that if you once suffer women to eat of the tree of knowledge, the rest of the family will soon be reduced to the same kind of 'aerial and unsatisfactory diet.' *

But still there seems to be a curious want of balance in the present system of female middle-class education in this country, which devotes the first seventeen or eighteen years of a girl's life to the process of unfitting

---

* Sydney Smith.

her for the most useful duties of future years. So that, at one or two and twenty, when a French or American girl would be quite mistress of the science of domestic economy, an English one is just beginning to stumble through its first rudiments.

I do not say that English women are too highly educated. I do not see how this can be ; for why should not the finely tempered instrument receive the highest possible polish ? and why should powers which God has given be permitted to rust in idle sloth ? But I do say that, among the middle classes, they are not wisely educated, and that their practical and industrial training is not in proportion to their intellectual. From which fact arise many and serious evils ; though how these are to be remedied, on the present modelling of boarding and day schools, is not very easy to see.

Perhaps I have written too strongly ; but if so, it has been in the vivid rememberance of much discomfort and vexation, much waste of time and no little of money, which might have been spared to myself, by an earlier initiation into certain important mysteries. I have no doubt that aunt Margaret, had she been spared to us, would have forthwith proceeded to remedy this defect ; but she was gone, and for some time I contented myself with a merely nominal performance of my duties as housekeeper, leaving the burden of them to Betty, who liked this arrangement too well to find fault with it. And so long as she remained the pre-

siding genius of the parsonage kitchen, dinners came and
went without giving me more trouble than mushrooms
or blackberries.

But alas! Betty one day informed me that she was
about to follow aunt Margaret's example, and enter the
'blessed estate of matrimony.' And when she and her
large deal box were fairly off the premises, and I was
left with the brawny-wristed, red-haired damsel installed
as her successor, whose strong points seemed to consist
in breaking dishes and manufacturing leaden bread, then,
indeed, my troubles began in earnest.

I will not weary you by describing them, or tell how
my poor father meekly submitted to half-cooked meat,
impracticable pastry, and soups that had 'neither savour
nor salt,' until I had worked out for my guidance a few
simple rules, with which I ought to have been familiar
from the first.

But there were other problems, not so easily solved,
which the business of housekeeping pressed upon my
attention. It awoke me from my idealism to the perception that this every-day world, full of small cares and
homely duties, was very different from the dream-world
in which I had hitherto lived; and the want of harmony
between the two was a source of perpetual irritation.

I could discover no link of connection between the
study and the kitchen. The one was a white tent of
repose, whose stillness was broken only by muffled voices
from the far historic past, or by words of wisdom from

the thinkers of the present. The other was an un-genial region, where the 'perversity of inanimate matter' reigned supreme, and where my own hot temper was by no means kept under. The contrast jarred upon me very uncomfortably. Surely the different elements of which one's life is made up should blend in perfect union. But between these two there could be nothing but discord.

And yet another missing link occasioned me still more anxious thought. It might be possible, by dint of search, to discover one between the material and the in-tellectual; but there could be none, as it seemed to me, between the material and the spiritual. A thousand analogies might have taught me how to look for what I sought, and where to find it; but as yet my eyes were too dim to perceive them. And as I did not think of asking counsel in this matter from Him who 'giveth wisdom liberally' to all who lack, and should have deemed it irreverence to make such apparent trifles a subject of prayer, I stumbled on painfully in the dark for many months, because I failed to grasp a truth which was afterwards to turn 'earthly care into heavenly dis-cipline,' and shed a light not of this world upon all life's common things.

The first glimpse I gained of this wondrous alchemy, was from one whose friendship I count among God's choicest gifts. Indeed, I almost wonder how I can have proceeded thus far in my story without mentioning her name, unless it is that with these earlier years of which I have written she is not so closely associated.

About a mile from Heatherstone, in a low, rambling cottage, full of quaint corners and gables, and roofed with mantling ivy, there lived a lady, to whom I believe I was first introduced in the complicated array of cambric and lace, which is supposed proper to the very earliest stage of baby life. So, of course, I cannot remember the time when I did not know Miss Melville; and, as a child, I used to think of her as belonging to some very remote antiquity, somehow contemporary with Queen Elizabeth and Joan of Arc, and various other historic and unhistoric personages, whose images flitted through my fancy in rather incongruous procession. But she must have been quite young when I was a little girl, for, at the time of which I write, she was barely more than forty.

I often looked with envy on the life which seemed such a ceaseless ministry of kindness, though I could not help shrinking a little from the thought of its entire solitude; for Miss Melville lived at Ivyburn alone, and seemed to have 'nobody belonging to her.' One by one all closer ties had fallen away, and she was left, as she sometimes laughingly said, 'a nun without vows.' Sometimes I used to wonder whether this was the future her girlish dreams had pictured. I rather fancied not.

But what a benefit it was to the community in general,

and to all who might be in any trouble in particular, that Anne Melville had remained all her life an unclaimed blessing ! for she was always at leisure to help, and always ready to sympathise—a true daughter of consolation, strong, and calm, and tender. Her voice was low and full, with a sort of muffled power in its deep, musical tones ; and the sunshine of smiles which had so often lighted up her face, seemed to linger there even when the features were at rest.

She was a sensible, practical wóman, moreover, clever and capable, possessing what the Americans call 'faculty,' and knowing how to use it,—a little conscious of her power, perhaps a little determined in her prejudices, as persons of strong character are apt to be, and perhaps a trifle wedded to her particular modes of thinking and acting. But then there are spots in the sun; and which of us is wholly free from fault? In her younger days she must have been handsome, and the noble presence and fine moulding of the features still remained, though early bloom had faded.

After aunt Margaret's marriage, Miss Melville did all in her power to supply her place as my friend and counsellor. Indeed, I think she was kind to all young girls. Standing herself on solid ground, amidst the quiet afternoon shadows, she looked back with loving, wistful eyes, to those who were still tossed and struggling on uncertain waters ; and it seemed a part of her appointed work to reach towards them a helping hand, and speak a word of earnest cheer. Her own girlhood, with its strivings after an unattainable ideal, and the inevitable sadness of its failure, lay not so far behind but that it was still fresh in her memory; and I think her quick instinct discerned in me the token of some similar struggles.

But I kept myself rather aloof from her, standing on the defensive, with a mixture of pride and shyness; for at that wise period I was a little given to depreciate feminine friendships, and to think the society of women, except that of Mary Wilton, extremely uninteresting.

So Miss Melville quietly waited and watched, trying to link my life to her own in many little unnoticed ways; but never forcing herself upon me, or making violent demonstrations of friendship. And thus at length she gained her point; and I gave her the love which we give to few, though those few are kept 'under our own life's key;' and to her, as we sat at work together one afternoon in early autumn—the second autumn after my return from school—I unburdened some of my troubles.

My father had gone to attend the Visitation at White-haven, and I was spending the day at Ivyburn, that I might help Miss Melville in making divers small garments for an unwelcome twin, which had recently arrived in the village. We had been stitching away for a time in silence, for my thoughts persisted in dwelling upon some domestic grievance which had disturbed me that morning, and I fear I must have given my good hostess so many pre-occupied answers, that at length she was fain to leave me in peace. But looking up once, I met her penetrating gaze fixed upon me, with a question in it which I felt must be answered.

'Dear Miss Melville, I must apologize for being so quiet and stupid, but really—'

'What is the matter, my dear child? You have sighed three several times within the last five minutes.'

'Have I? I was quite unconscious of it. But I believe I get tired now and then. There is so much to think of. One has to keep such a lot of small machinery going, and there are so many wheels and pins to look after.'

'But, Elsie, what would you do if you had a crowd of children, like Mrs Preston, for instance, and a baby every year?'

I shook my head at this picture, which was almost too appalling to contemplate. 'But the worst of it is, Miss Melville, that the machinery doesn't work after all. I believe housekeepers are like poets—born, not made; and I certainly wasn't born one. Besides, what does it signify?'

'I should think it signified a great deal.'

'But why?'

'Principally because it's a woman's duty.'

'That's conclusive, certainly. But, Miss Melville, I don't think the idea of duty has ever been strongly developed in my mind.   I don't know; I suppose it must be my own fault; but mere duty always seems to me rather drudgery.'

'Yes, and mere duty always must be.   But there is room here for love as well as duty ; and where there is love, there is freedom and delight.'

I looked inquiringly, for the words sounded strange to me ; some tones within were silent which should have made up the harmony between the speaker and myself. But Miss Melville went on—

'I think your mistake lies here, Elsie, does it not, that you look upon these household cares as something that must be done apart from Christ, something that takes you away from all companionship with Him during so many hours of every day ?   But is it not rather true that all this our earthly work finds a place in our offering of love to Christ ?   Can we not find even here, among these merely material things, a link to draw us into communion with Him ?   We may climb to His presence otherwise than by sunbeams;* for St Paul tells us, "to do all in the name of the Lord Jesus;" and we are surely commanded in "everything by prayer and supplication, to let our requests be made known unto Him."   It is only when we do this, that we can expect to have our hearts and minds "kept in the peace of God."'

I made no reply at the time, but I pondered much

---

* 'Then by a sunbeam I will climb to Thee.'—*George Herbert.*

and deeply. Here was a glimpse into a world of whose very existence I had never dreamed. This communion with Christ; this longing to find in everything a link to His presence,—here was something I did not understand. For as yet I was young in the heavenly life ; and though I knew Christ as my Saviour, I had not recognised Him as my Friend. But that night, in my quiet little room, I prayed in His name, 'That which I see not, teach Thou me.'

And the answer came,—not then, nor all at once, but slowly, and, as it were, imperceptibly. God puts a thread into our hands, and bids us follow it ; and in doing so faithfully, we learn the secrets of His will.

Such a thread—slender, but sure—were Miss Melville's words to me. They taught me that fellowship with the Father and the Son can cast a glory over life's common cares. They nerved me to take up the one cross which lay in my path ; because I saw that, although no other would recognise it as such, I might count surely on His sympathy, who had once been tempted even as I. I might 'go and tell Jesus'—might lean on His arm, and, so leaning, I should be strong.

Henceforth drudgery was over. There was interest even in housekeeping, for it was part of the work which He had given. And so long as I held fast this remembrance, I dared not ask for anything else ; for those words seemed to rebuke me, 'Whatsoever *He* saith unto you, *do it.*'

And I learned,—though, alas! how slowly, and with how many intervals of forgetfulness!—that the submission which accepts its daily task, and looks for no other, is itself service.

IV.

A SABBATH OF REST.

'Happy is he who heareth
  The signal of his release,
In the bells of the Holy City
  The chimes of eternal peace.'

CHAPTER IV.

A SABBATH OF REST.

ND so the days passed on, for the most part very quietly, and with little to mark their progress. They seem to me now like a distant, shadowy shore,— a land where it was always afternoon'—filled with a dreamy slumberous light. But perhaps that is only because I look back to them across the wide sea of years, and the pressure of some nearer cares prevents the remembrance of those which are past.

Mary Wilton, who had left school before me—for she was two years older than I,—was now filling her place as the eldest daughter of a large family. All were younger than herself; for Mary had reached her seventh year before her quiet nursery was invaded by other pairs of little feet, restless as hers had never been,—which pattered their way in a month through more shoes than she had worn in six.   So Mary was fully occupied, and I saw her but seldom.

Yet, when we did meet, we generally found that, though from opposite sides, and by distinct processes of thought, we had arrived at the same mental results, which were to be in their turn, perhaps, thrown down among the heap of things forgotten, or only used as stepping-stones for the obtaining of others.

And in higher hopes we were entirely one, though Mary's hold of these was always firmer far than mine.   I think she must have been very young when her spirit first found its true home and rest, and learned to 'worship at the temple's inner shrine.'

But about the time of which I write, when I had nearly attained my twentieth year, and Mary, as I have said, was two years older, I was conscious that a change had come over her, easy to perceive, though difficult to define.   It was like the flush of green which the breath of spring brings over field and wood ; like the trembling, dewy light, which breaks at sunrise over the landscape, lying grey and still in the shadow of the dawn.   It came quietly, mysteriously, but it touched and glorified her whole being.   Her nature seemed deepened, her sympathies awakened.   There was brighter colour on her cheek—a shy, wistful light in the clear grey eye.   But in time the colour faded, the light died out.   And now there grew a weary look upon the face, and often a tone, half sad, half fretful, in the voice which often smote painfully upon my heart.

Should I try to comfort her? Better not, perhaps. I had little of sorrow's teaching myself at that time; but still, an instinctive feeling taught me that there are battles which must be fought and won alone, and wounds which a human touch would only irritate. And I could see, by the rigid lines of her pale, stedfast face, that Mary had set herself to suffer and be silent.

And did she succeed? What will a woman's pride not succeed in? But I think success was dearly bought, for her nature seemed a little hardened by the discipline to which she subjected it. Suffering, not shared, but concealed and struggled with, has, in some characters, a tendency to blunt sympathy. Insensibly she seemed to draw further off from the common life around her—from common cares, and joys, and sorrows; looking down upon them a little coldly, a little sadly, as things in which she had no part. A touch of frost had fallen upon the clear, calm heart. Would it melt again? Would she become merely an estimable woman, good and useful in her measure, but neither winning nor sympathetic? Or would the hardness melt in God's good time, and the sealed-up tide of love and tenderness flow forth once more?

This question, though not perhaps in words expressed, was much upon my mind, when Mary surprised me by coming to Heatherstone for a visit of a week. She wanted rest, she said; and indeed she looked weary enough,—as if the mind, in its intensity of suffering and endurance, was wearing away the body. For the first few days she hardly spoke, but would lie listlessly on the sofa, or wander in the garden, till my heart ached to see her. And yet I could do nothing. It seemed the greatest kindness to let her alone. But after this she roused herself. Surely the one true Comforter had drawn near to her, as He so often does in that silence of a great sorrow, which is like the shadow of His own presence!

My birthday befell while she was with us. It was on the 27th of October, just when our noble hills and woods were beginning to exchange their kingly robing for the winter drapery of brown and black. It had been a true autumn day—very fair, with a touch of sadness, one of those whose subtle influence blends unconsciously with many a future year ; a pure well-spring of delight, though hidden away under a heap of life's dust and cobwebs. And we had spent it mostly out of doors, coming home in the growing twilight not a little tired.

The servant met me with the unusual announcement that 'the master' was not well, and had gone to lie down. I went up to his room at once, with a strange dread upon my mind. He had seemed quite well when we met at our early dinner ; but I knew it would be no trifling ailment which would induce him to break up our happy trio on this the evening of my birthday. Yet, when I saw him, I could find nothing to fear. He had a headache, he said, but quiet and a cup of tea would cure it; I must apologise to Miss Wilton for his absence, and he hoped we should enjoy the evening together. So, after taking him some tea, and watching him drink it, I left him to rest, having made all the arrangements I could think of for his comfort.

Mary and I had much happy talk that evening. Some things we said have been stereotyped on my mind ever since: words lightly spoken, but which the future was to invest with a strange significance. We had been comparing, as we often did, our separate lives, which outwardly possessed so few points of contact; hers full of the freshness and busy stir of family life, and widening ever into new channels of interest and sympathy; mine flowing in a very narrow current.

'There isn't enough in it to keep me from stagnation,' I exclaimed abruptly, giving utterance at last to a lurking discontent, which had been seething in my heart for months, and which had led me away from the peace of accepting God's will, into the restlessness of struggling against it. 'Sometimes I feel as if I could hardly breathe in this pent-up nook. There is a troublesome amount of energy somewhere in my composition, which is always crying out for more work than it can get.'

Mary looked up and smiled. I believe she had never been troubled with more energy than she could manage; for her physical frame was not robust, and every exertion demanded an effort of will stronger than a person in full health could possibly understand. So she could hardly comprehend the strong impulses which made me thus restless, where she would have kept the 'even tenor of her way' in full content. But she did not answer me, and I went on.

'I want to *do* something in the world. I get tired of study that ends in nothing. It seems to me entirely resultless and selfish.'

'But surely it need not be, Elsie. I remember, though, how that difficulty used to haunt me when I first left school; rose up like a vexing ghost, whenever I ventured to take an hour for mental improvement.'

'Well, how did you lay it at last?'

'I began to see that no culture can be too high for the work we have to do, and that only the furnished and disciplined mind can have any power of useful influence.'

'But that seems a kind of working in the dark.'

'Is it not true of many things, that we walk by faith, not by sight? We may acquire one bit of knowledge after another, in obedience to what seems a blind craving, but we believe that it will *fit in*, and fill up a corner some day. And oh! Elsie,' she added, with the bright look which often made her calm face positively beautiful, 'may we not rejoice to lay a polished instrument at God's feet, though only His hand can put the edge upon it.'

'Yes, I suppose you are right. At any rate just now I have nothing to take the place of study. If only women might have a profession as well as men—'

'We should not be gainers, Elsie. I think a woman would be always less of a woman in proportion as she was more of an artist or a physician. Men can take up a profession, and keep *themselves* out of it; follow it as something apart. But we must be absorbed by whatever we do; possessed by it in fact, if we are to gain any true mastery over it; and in that case what is to become of our own duties in our own homes?'

'What if we have no homes?' I asked, losing sight of myself for a moment, and getting an odd glimpse of a great social problem which is now pressing painfully for solution. 'But I only meant some women, Mary. I don't believe you want a profession at all. That easy, home-life satisfies you as it does many. You don't know what it is to look at the work of the world, and grow feverish because you can't throw yourself into it.'

Mary shook her head. The duties which seemed to me, perhaps because I did not understand their true significance, at once difficult, and yet too small to satisfy my eager longings, were all she had ever asked for; often more than she felt she could accomplish.

Now, although I spoke in impatience and forgetfulness of Him who had appointed my work as well as my home, I believe that such words may find an echo in the hearts of many who have His guiding in reverent remembrance. In me they were dictated by an evil demon of discontent, which I should have sought to cast out by prayer; but there are thousands whose spirits

D

beat as painfully as mine against the bars of a mere young lady life—not necessarily idle, but aimless and desultory, who would be both healthier and happier, if the leisure, which remains after the faithful satisfaction of every relative claim, were filled up by some work of head or hand, whether of practical effort for others, or of independent labour for themselves.

And so the evening passed. Mary's figure is before me even now, rising in clear outlines over all the years that lie between. Even her dress I recollect—of some soft neutral tint, brightened by a dainty little knot of blue ribbon, tied under the white collar. Towards nine o'clock the autumn wind rose suddenly, and moaned among the trees outside, dashing the withered leaves against the window panes. We heard it in the pauses of our talk ; and I remember that Mary shivered nervously, as if the sound awoke some responsive chords within, which answered with a start and thrill.

Before we separated for the night, I crept up softly to my father's room, and opened the door as noiselessly as possible. He seemed to rouse from an uneasy sleep, and answered me at first confusedly, as if he mistook me for some one else. But in a minute or two his consciousness returned, and he looked at me with an expression of wistful, earnest tenderness, which is as vividly before me now as if I had seen it only yesterday. One look, no more, and then he sank off to sleep again.

I went down stairs to despatch a messenger for Dr

Wilton, returning immediately to take up my position in the sick-room. Carlo's successor, a grey terrier, with eyes that, in their dark depths, showed a look of almost human intelligence, stretched himself at the foot of the bed to share my watch. There was silence in the house —silence that seemed to shiver and creep in its intensity, —unbroken, save by the ticking of the clock, or a soft step on the stair now and then, when Mary glided into the room to see if she could in any way help me.

There are no songs for us in nights of darkness like this, unless God gives them; but I remember the word which was brought to me then by unseen ministry, to quiet the trembling of heart which nothing else would have reached: 'I sought the Lord, and he heard me, and delivered me from all my fears.' I often think that verse is one of the touches of God's hand, which falls exactly upon the place where our weakness is greatest. For is it not often true that our fears are the heaviest part of our burden, that which most of all crushes and oppresses us? So that, in delivering us from them by the strengthened faith, which is His gift, God supplies the deepest need of His people, and 'gives them the victory' their own weakness could never have gained. And even although 'the thing which we greatly fear may come upon us,' that victory is still ours; for our eyes are opened now to see the chastening rod, as a token of our Father's loving remembrance, and although we still shrink and quiver when the stroke falls, we *fear* it no longer.

Dr Wilton came at length. He said little; indeed he was never a man of many words, and his command of feature and voice was so complete that I could not gain much from the study of either. Nevertheless, by a kind of spirit-instinct, I gathered that his opinion was not favourable—

> 'And my heart sank within me, as in wells
>   The waters sink before an earthquake's shock.'

Dr Wilton advised me to get some one to help in nursing, and would fain have taken Mary away with him that night; but she begged to be allowed to remain until the next day.

But the morning brought little change. 'Shall I send for Ernest?' I asked, when I had followed Dr Wilton to the dining-room after his morning visit. He hesitated a moment, not, I felt sure, from any uncertainty, but from a kindly wish to save me pain.

'Yes, I think you had better; or stay, I'll write a line myself.'

'How soon can he be here?'

'This is Thursday: not possible before Saturday night, perhaps Sunday morning.' For the iron road had not crossed Shap Fell in those days, and tidings of joy or grief were not flashed to human hearts so rapidly as now.

I turned to bid Mary goodbye; but our adieus were taken in silence, except for the pressure of lips and hands, which spoke a whole heartful. And in her place came

Miss Melville, always ready at the call of need; and Mrs Smith, an elderly woman from the village, was a most efficient nurse. But, indeed, there was little nursing required. The dear invalid lay for the most part in a kind of stupor that was not sleep, only rousing up now and then to take a few spoonfulls of nourishment. He spoke little, but murmured low words of prayer, or called softly for the dead wife whose memory he had always held in such tender keeping. He seemed to know me too, and once, as I knelt by his side, he laid his hand gently on my head, as if in silent blessing. How often, since then, I have seemed to feel that touch upon my brow!

Ernest, to my intense joy, arrived on Saturday night. The next morning rose clear and fair, the air filled with that peculiar, brooding stillness, so often perceptible in the country on the Day of Rest. Ernest and I were in the sick-room together, both feeling, though neither acknowledged to the other, that our watch there would not be long. The bell of our little Church, where the morning service was taken by a neighbouring clergyman, broke suddenly upon the silence, and its quivering vibrations seemed to penetrate even the dull ears that were fast closing to all earthly sound. My father looked up and recognised us both with his characteristic smile, that was always singularly sweet and bright.

' It must be Church time,' he said ; · 'but I cannot go this morning. What day of the month is it, Elsie ?'

'The 1st of November,' I replied, with a quick remembrance that it was All Saints' Day. And taking up a Bible which lay at hand, I turned to the glorious passage appointed for the epistle. And even as I read of the great multitude which no man can number, who stand before the throne and before the Lamb, the freed spirit passed beyond the river, and Ernest and I were orphans.

V.

TRANSPLANTING.

‘ I see around me here
Things which you cannot see.   We die, my friend ;
Nor we alone ; but that which each man loved
And prized, in his peculiar nook of earth,
Dies with him, or is changed.’

—The Excursion.

CHAPTER V.

TRANSPLANTING.

ALL was over at last. All which love could do was done, and the consciousness of this gave grief a new bitterness. It is not till our dead are buried out of our sight, that we feel how completely they have gone from us ; nothing left to us but memory, and the relics which it holds so dear. Then come the moments of desolation and utter loneliness, and often, too, of mental and physical exhaustion, when we can do nothing but bend, chilled and helpless, beneath the dull weight of our sorrow,—only looking up, out of our dumb agony, to recognise it as a companion for life, from whose presence we can never be free. Do we not all know the terrible anguish of those first days of bereavement, when the storm, which has wrecked our dearest hopes, is

followed by a calm, yet more strange and dark? Well
for us, if we can hear in both the voice of Him

'Who made the darkness and the light,
And dwells not in the light alone.'

What my father had been to me, no one ever knew.
There was a secret sympathy between us, subtile and
strong, though always unspoken. I felt that he understood me, as no one else ever did. His spirit knew the
measure of mine. His kindly eyes had read, at a glance,
what other people would not have comprehended after a
week's explanation. I always had from him the tenderest
consideration, the most gentle shielding. And now he
was gone—gone—and his place could never be filled;
my heart went after him with a wild, passionate yearning,
which seemed as if it must bring him back, even from
the very grave.

But the routine of life does not stand still when a
great sorrow comes, though, in our first shock and
bewilderment, we almost expect that it will. We who
have lived through many trials, know that grief must
sometimes be put aside for a while, by mere force of
determination; not reasoned against, and not as yet
comforted, but simply *made to wait.* It may come by
and by; but it must first learn to bide its time. Howbeit,
this wisdom is not learned in a day, and to me it came
but slowly, though I was obliged of course, to exert myself; for Heatherstone Parsonage could be my home no

longer, and there were many affairs to be wound up within a short space.

It was another great trial, this leaving the old home; for to me the quaint brown house had almost assumed a sort of personality. The creak of every door, the rattle of every window, even the turn of the staircase, and the sound of the bells, had become a part of my inner consciousness. They were present to me when memory struggled with the twilight of infancy; they were associated with many an hour of love and sorrow since then; and I could hardly picture to myself a life in which these outward surroundings should have no place.

But still it must be. And the question pressed imperatively for an answer, whither should I go when I left Heatherstone? My father had left us little worldly wealth; for his living was very small, and Ernest's education had been expensive. For me there were a few hundreds, safely invested,—enough to fall back upon in case of need, but not enough to keep me above it. Evidently I must do something for myself.

But what? I discussed this point very seriously with Miss Melville, during a short stay with her; while Ernest was obliged to leave me for a few days, before our final departure. For he wished me to remain with him in Liverpool for a time, to 'make his lodging look like home.'

'And then, I suppose, I must become a governess,

or keep a school, or something of that sort,' I said to my kind hostess, as we sat together one evening, in the crimson glow of the fire, before the lamp was lighted.

'Not necessarily, my dear. I know that is the first thing to which people's thoughts turn. But unless they have some special fondness for teaching and for children, I think they had much better do something else; for there will be no success in work for which there is no love; and it is the worse for herself and her pupils if a woman turns educator when she is not fitted to be one.'

'I am fond of children,' I said; 'but I don't think I have the gift of imparting knowledge.'

'You hardly know whether or not you possess a gift till you come to exercise it; but if you undertake anything for which you are really not suited, you degrade yourself far more than if you were to begin to sweep floors or take in washing.'

'But, Miss Melville, there are so few things that women can do.'

'There you are wrong, Elsie. There are many things that a woman can do, if she will only set about them.'

'Well; but what things?'

Twenty years later, Miss Melville might have answered this question more readily. She might have told me of law-copying, for instance, or photograph tinting and printing, or engraving on wood; but at that time, though she saw clearly the need of more varied employment for women, she could not point to its actual provision.

'I only wish,' she said, musingly, 'that every girl were taught how to do something with her fingers or her head, which might be a property to her for life, instead of wasting so much time in learning what she can seldom turn to practical account. But I think it will be your best plan, my dear, if you really feel that teaching is not the work you would choose, to go to your brother for a while, as he proposes ; for, in a large town like Liverpool, you will more readily hear of some suitable employment, than in a place like this. And remember always the Christians privilege of resting in a promise, as sweet as true : "The Lord shall guide thee continually."'

She laid her hands caressingly on my hair as she said this ; for I was in my favourite position, curled up on the floor at her side.

'But, Miss Melville, have I a right to that promise ?'

'Surely, dear child ! Is not the prayer yours : "Order my steps in thy word ?"'

'Yes, oh yes ; but still—'

'Still you did not expect it would be answered. Ah! Elsie, how few of us could bear the response, "According to your faith be it unto you !" But it is *true*,' she added earnestly, speaking rather to herself than to me ; 'God's guidance is *always* given, though I do not say that it is always given speedily. People talk sometimes as if one had nothing to do but look up into the sky, and see it written there ; but that is not true. Generally, I think, God disciplines our faith through our patience, by making us wait His time,—not in the light, which would be easy, but in the darkness, which is often very dreary. "Light is *sown* for the righteous." It does not immediately appear,, but it is sure in the end ; and "though it tarry, wait."'

I saw Mary Wilton but once more before my departure for Liverpool. She spent a short winter's day with me at Ivyburn ; and with her (for I could have borne no other companionship) I paid my last visit to my parents' grave. There was a look of pain upon her face as we turned away, which showed me that her unspoken grief might, after all, be more bitter than mine. For there is a sense in which death may divide us from those we love less entirely than life. It gives us those whom it takes. They are ours more truly than many who are left.

I had but little communication with aunt Margaret since her marriage. Her letters, frequent at first, came now at long intervals, and were sadly changed in tone, —showing, by their subdued hopelessness, that the writer had joined that pale army of 'martyrs by the pang without the palm,' of whom there are so many in this sorrowful world. 'She would gladly have offered me a home,' she said, 'but circumstances forbade it.' Of course they did ! It would have been impossible for me and Mr Merton ever to live together in peace.

But, putting this aside, I was determined to owe the means of subsistence to no one. If I had been old, or in delicate health, the case would have been different; but God had given me youth and strength, and why should I not work? So my answer was quite decided, when Ernest urged that his income, now an increasing one—for he had a rapidly rising practice as a solicitor,—would suffice amply for us both.

'It is not right that I should be a mere weight upon your wheels, when, as we used to say together on Sunday evenings long ago, I can "learn and labour truly to get mine own living." Besides, you may marry, and then—'

'Nonsense!' he replied, laughing; but his lips, always much given to making unconscious revelations, contradicted this concise answer. And, as I looked at his handsome figure, and bright sunshiny face, where truth and nobleness might be read at a glance, I thought he would have no great difficulty in finding a wife. Might she only be worthy of him!

I bade adieu to Heatherstone in exactly six weeks from the time of my dear father's death. The parsonage had already become the abode of his successor; and I could hardly bear to remain in the neighbourhood, and see my old home in the possession of a stranger. Very foolish, you will say. Very foolish, reader; but, I fear me, you will never understand one half of a woman's nature, if you must needs be so excessively sensible.

Carlo was left with Miss Melville, to whom, poor fellow, he was very slow in transferring his allegiance. But she won him at last, as she had won his mistress— over whom her wise, womanly influence was only strengthened by distance and time.

VI.

WHAT CAME OF A ROLL OF PARCHMENT.

'O'er the fields of earth lie scattered
    Noble fruitage and blossoms rare ;
Yon city the store has gathered,
    And the garner of hearts is there.'

BONAR.

E

CHAPTER VI.

WHAT CAME OF A ROLL OF PARCHMENT.

OWN life seemed at first very strange, and not entirely pleasant. Ernest was the only person I knew in the whole city, and he was necessarily absent in his office during a great part of every day. I began to understand the truth of what Bacon somewhere says, that 'a crowd is not company, and faces are but a gallery of pictures, and talk but a tinkling cymbal, where there is no love.' I had never felt so solitary among the Cumberland hills, as now in the 'crowded loneliness' of Liverpool. Man was no nearer, and nature had gone farther off. And, for a time, I could not help feeling as if God were farther off too.

But I am sure the change was in many ways for good. It was something new for me to feel around me the stirring of intellectual activity; something new, and very healthful, to be pulled forcibly out of my own narrow groove of thought, and shown that there were 'more things in heaven and earth' than had been dreamt of in my small philosophy. I learned more from the living lore of the city, than even from nature and books in my quiet country home. They are valuable teachers both; but the contact of mind with mind, in 'yonder social mill,' is something yet better.

Then, again, the town discipline of interruptions was not without its use. I had been accustomed to move on in my own beaten track, giving so much time to one thing, so much to another, without consulting the pleasure or convenience of any one, and growing not a little self-absorbed and impatient in consequence. I was to learn now, first the duty, and then the delight, of taking my work as it came,—giving up some cherished plan without vexation, and accepting a task I had not chosen, as my heavenly Master's assigning, even when it took the shape of what seemed to me a hindrance. And this is one of the great lessons of a woman's life,—the only one, I think, which effectually counteracts that small selfishness, which is so apt to spread itself over characters otherwise both noble and beautiful.

And, after a while, I saw that God might be as near in the city as in the village:

> 'Thy power and love, my love and trust,
>   Make one place everywhere.'

But the winter passed, and the early spring as well,

before Ernest would permit me to enter upon my search for employment. Indeed, for some time I needed not to seek it farther than in his wardrobe, which presented dismal traces of the helplessness of masculine fingers in the matter of necessary repairs. So, for a time, I was employed in the diligent following of what some one calls 'woman's plough,'—a little instrument for which I am old-fashioned enough to retain a great respect, partly because, in addition to other excellences, I think its peaceful motion has no small power in repairing inequalities of temper, as well as deficiencies in raiment. I have pricked many restless thoughts into wristband and seam, which might else have been apt to find less innocent expression.

But when rents had been darned, and buttons and strings persuaded into their places, I began to find my unoccupied time a little heavy.

'What can you do, Birdie?' said Ernest one day, when I had expressed my intention of going down to town to 'seek my fortune.' 'Stay here, and sing to me.'

'I won't, unless you let me work. Men ought not to usurp the privilege of being bread-winners.'

'Nay, Elsie ; I only thought of sparing you.'

'I know—I know.' My arms were round his neck in a moment, repentant and appealing. 'But you would leave me to die of idleness, as half the women in the world do.'

'Well then, to save you from a fate so tragic, what is

to be done? I suppose you decline entirely the teaching department?'

'Yes; it is not *in me* to be a first-rate governess, and an inferior one I don't choose to be.'

'Then what will you be? Let us go through the list of your qualifications. Can you keep accounts?'

I shook my head, for the old childish dread of figures was strong upon me still. I knew 'five times five' in the multiplication table, but, beyond that, the ground was uncertain.

Ernest looked grave. 'It's a curious thing that you women are brought up in such entire ignorance of the science of quantity. A great pity, too; for a good accountant can always command her worth. So that is set aside. Then, what *can* you do, Elsie?'

A question more easily asked than answered. My powers seemed to be gradually melting away, in the presence of an actual demand upon them. It is a great misfortune, in the education of women, that we are seldom furnished with any practical standard by which to measure our own deficiencies, of which we only become aware when it is too late to remedy them. For, when we pass beyond the receptive stage of life, new mental possessions are not readily gained. If the spring sowing is neglected, the growth of the later year is never luxuriant,—a truth which holds good in mental as well as material husbandry.

'I have it,' said Ernest, looking up from a profound

study of the carpet with the light of a new thought breaking over his face; 'I'll bring you some work when I come from the office to-morrow.'

'What sort of work,' I asked, wonderingly.

'Never mind, little curiosity! Learn patience in the meantime.'

Which I tried to do; and, after he had gone to town the next morning, set forth on a country ramble, the better to exercise it. For, at first, I was disposed to be a little scornful of this same Lancashire 'country,' with its flat surface and unbroken horizon-line. Very tame it seemed, even commonplace, after the glory of form and colour which spreads itself over my beloved north. And, as nature will only reveal herself to loving eyes, and to hearts that receive with reverence her homeliest teachings, my pride robbed me of much refreshment, and made the daily walk rather an affair of duty than an occasion of thanksgiving; since I failed, for a long time, to perceive that in every bit of tangled hedge or moss-grown wall, there was enough to fill me with wonder and delight.

Our home was in what is now a mere suburb of Liverpool, but was then a tolerably quiet village, which the town had not yet overtaken with its outstretching arms. We had pleasant lodgings, though our rooms were small, and permitted us little more freedom of loco-motion than a fly may be supposed to enjoy in a spider's web! But our ambition was small too, and in those days crinoline was not!

Moreover, the house stood in a kind of court, containing a few poplars and a mountain ash, on whose bright berries there seemed to rest a gleam of sunshine from dearer skies. Ernest said it kept a breath of the hills among its rustling leaves.

I watched for my brother's return that evening with some eagerness, being curious to see what shape the promised 'work' might assume. It came, to my surprise, in that of a roll of parchment, which he laid before me with a mischievous smile.

'There is my promise, Birdie; what do you think of it?'

'Why, Ernest, what have I to do with rolls of parchment?'

'Just what I wish to explain. The truth is, Elsie, I am going to teach you law-copying; and, when you have mastered it, you shall have the same salary I pay my copying-clerk. You will hardly become an expert copyist in less than six months; but you may begin to earn money in a shorter time than that.'

'So long?' I asked in my simplicity. 'What difficulty can there be in learning to write in one way rather than another?'

'Give me some tea, Elsie, and then you shall try it.'

So I did 'try it,' and speedily found my mistake, being compelled to acknowledge that this art of crabbed writing must be acquired with as much pains and care as any other. But I set to work with great zeal and diligence, receiving a fresh lesson every evening, and practising, during the day, what I had already learned; so that, before the end of summer, my teacher pronounced himself well content with my progress. He was able to keep me in full employment, and to satisfy all my scruples on the score of payment, by the assurance that, but for my services, he would have been obliged to engage an additional clerk. So I took the salary he offered—about £1 per week,—and felt quite rich upon it, paying my share, though not a full one, of our joint. outlay, and saving a small overplus from my personal expenses.

It is true, the work was rather uninteresting; and now and then I felt as if my mind, as well as my fingers, were growing cramped by constant contact with the legal technicalities, to which I could attach so little meaning. But even through these I could often feel the strong beat of a living heart, with its mysteries of joy and woe, and sometimes, too, of crime; so they were not entirely without interest. Besides, they seemed to be the work assigned me; and remembering, with tears, my recent terrible lesson upon discontent, I dared not permit myself to murmer either against daily duty or daily bread. The 'wider life' for which I asked, in my blindness, had not been given; for how many are the prayers which our Father mercifully refuses to grant, or answers them by contraries! But He was teaching me, instead, a lesson of deeper trust in Himself, and more simple acceptance of His appointment ; leading me thus gradually into that secret of submission and self-surrender, our initiation into which is, I think, the true sacrament of the Christian life.

> 'One prayer I have—all prayers in one—
>   When I am wholly Thine;
> Thy will, my God, Thy will be done;
>   And may that will be mine.'

VII.

NEW FRIENDS.

'A maiden, mild and beautiful,
    And grave beyond her years,
With eyes of dreamy sunshine full,
    But not too bright for tears.'
                    —*Hebrew Children.*

CHAPTER VII.

NEW FRIENDS.

ONE day—it was nearly two years after I had left Heatherstone, though I found it hard to believe that so much time had really passed—I had occasion to go to Liverpool on a shopping expedition. This, by the way, is a business in which we women are supposed to delight—one of the many slanders which we endure in meek silence, having learned, by experience, that counter assertion has little power to influence any masculine estimate of our likes and dislikes, which is always so much more correct than our own knowledge of the same!

And shopping on this particular occasion had been more than usually unpleasant. It was November— November with its dreary winds and murky atmosphere; and even Liverpool, the bright city by the waters, looked very dismal and dark, as seen through such a medium; for a fog had settled upon the town, raw, damp, and penetrating, full of sore throat, and bronchitis, and all manner of evil.

I was returning to Wavertree by omnibus, congratulating myself that the day was over, and looking forward to the evening, with its warmth, and light, and pleasant converse; for we were very happy together, Ernest and I,—brother and sister, not in name only, but in the love which does not always accompany the outward bond. He was sitting opposite to me now, for by this omnibus he usually came up from town; and, looking at him, and at the fireside picture which filled my mental vision, I had not paid much heed to my fellow-passengers, until I heard a remarkably sweet voice request to be set down 'opposite Edgehill Church.'

There was the slightest possible tinge of Scotch in the accent, but it was Scotch the purest and most refined; evidently spoken by a lady, and given with singular clearness and delicacy of tone. Involuntarily I turned to look at the speaker, and to discern, if possible, what sort of features went with this voice. But they were hidden by a thick veil, and I could catch only a gleam of white teeth as the stranger bent forward to take up a small parcel she had dropped, and which Ernest was just then handing to her. They spoke, to my surprise, as if they had met before, and I was still further astonished when, having reached Edgehill Church, he started up to hand her out, treading on divers toes as he did so. Who could she be, this unknown maiden? That soft voice, with its silvery articulation, did not seem likely to belong to any one much in the habit of travelling by omnibus; and yet there she was, and where else could Ernest have met with her?

However, I kept my speculations to myself till we reached home, and were comfortably seated in our snug drawing-room, looking at one another through a kind of vista formed by the two mould candles which, in those days, supplied for us the place of gas. And then I asked, woman-like, as if the thought had only just occurred to me—

'By the way, Ernest, who was the lady you were polite enough to hand out of the omnibus at Edgehill?'

'Mrs Claude's governess,' he answered, with an indifference of manner and voice which did not conceal the bright gleam in his eyes. 'She lives at Everton, and generally comes up by that omnibus. You'll meet her on Friday, Elsie; for Mrs Claude asked me, when I called to-day, if we could not drink tea with them that evening.'

Mr Claude was the gentleman with whom Ernest had been articled, and he and his gentle, fascinating wife, were almost our only friends in Liverpool.

'But she will not be there, this Miss—— What is her name, Ernest?'

'Miss Munroe. Why, yes, I rather think she will

(the naughty fellow, he knew it for a fact). Mrs Claude told me she was very anxious to persuade her invalid brother (he is a cripple, Elsie, and this girl supports him almost entirely) to spend an evening there, and the carriage is to be sent for him on Friday. I should think his sister would be with him.'

It seemed very probable; but I could have smiled at the extreme gravity to which Ernest's face was tutored as he discussed the point.

'Then they are orphans—Miss Munroe and her brother—like ourselves, Ernest?'

'Yes. Mrs Claude told me their history once. It's the old story of reverses. Their father was a surgeon, I believe, and had a tolerable practice at Earn, some queer little outlandish town in the north of Scotland, when he was unfortunately induced to remove to Liverpool, under the impression that, in a wider sphere, his talents would be better appreciated. Poor fellow! he struggled on bravely with difficulties and discouragements for eleven years, and at length, when he was just beginning to see his way through them, he was carried off by typhoid fever, and these children were left in little more than poverty. But Miss Munroe at once became governess for Mrs Claude's children, and I think she has employment three afternoons in the week beside. Mrs Claude tells me she might have commanded several situations as resident governess, with high salary; but there is this poor, helpless brother whom she cannot leave.'

I could not help wondering whether all this information had been volunteered or elicited; but this was a point it did not seem wise to inquire into. Ernest went on—

'They live in a small house near Everton Church, because the invalid fancies he cannot breathe except on a hill top. I believe he does a little in wood-carving, which he was taught as a boy for amusement. You will go to Mrs Claude's on Friday, Elsie? She wants us to meet their clergyman, Mr Kenway—quite in your line; but I don't think any one else will be there. I promised you should go, for I know you like Mrs Claude, and so do I. One can't help seeing her to be thoroughly good, and yet she isn't in the least disagreeable. And, besides, I don't think it's good for you to shut yourself up with a bachelor brother, and see nothing of society.'

'How long a bachelor?' I asked; but the answer was a request for some tea.

Grace Munroe was in the drawing-room at Clayton Square when I entered it with Ernest on Friday evening, sitting a little apart, and hovered over by a cloud of children, of all ages and sizes, from *ones* upward; for it was still early, and, as our party was small, Mrs Claude would not have her little ones banished to the nursery. So, at first, I could hardly get a glimpse of her, and only caught now and then one of the musical tones which had arrested my attention at our first meeting.

F

Her brother, too, was there, half lost among cushions and sofa-rugs on a couch near the fire, which lighted up his pale features now and then with a glow almost like that of health.   Blue eyes, large and dreamy, a profusion of fair hair, and a mouth whose changeful curves and ceaseless play of expression one could never tire of watching; these I saw at the first glance, as well as the lines which years of pain and patience had traced on lip and brow.

We were not the latest arrival, for Mr and Mrs Kenway immediately followed us, with their daughter, a pretty little blonde, who floated about in an abundance of blue drapery, and looked the very impersonation of good-tempered insipidity.   Mrs Kenway I had met before; her husband for the first time this evening. They were a curious contrast these two—one full of the quietness of wisdom, the other not comprehending the wisdom of quietness.   Mrs Kenway was a woman of much bustle and energy, with overwhelming powers of chatter, and a capacity for general management which extended to every person and thing within her influence, her gentle, scholarly husband by no means excepted. I saw her bearing down upon me now from the other end of the room, and retreated among the children for shelter, taking on my knee a bundle of embroidery, in blue sash and shoulder-knots, which was toddling, rather unsteadily, on a pair of feet so fat that the tiny red shoes seemed in imminent danger of bursting.

'Are you fond of children?' asked the silvery voice.

'Very,' I replied; 'only I never know exactly what to do with them.'

How strange this answer seems to me now! But I remember that, in those days, I was always shy and awkward with children, as if they were curious pieces of machinery, whose working I did not understand, and was afraid to meddle with. And with all my intense love, nay, almost reverence, for the little creatures who seem so near to God, it often pained me to feel that I had so small power to attract or amuse them. In proof whereof, the aforesaid bundle of embroidery slipped from my knee, and established itself at Grace's feet, gazing up shyly into the sweet face which bent down to smile at it.

For it *was* a sweet face, I could see that now, with its truthful eyes, and broad, open brow—the face of a true woman, with a look of repose and quiet power. And it was a face to be trusted; albeit the corners of the mouth betrayed a little lurking humour, not to say naughtiness. She was not like her brother, except in that unexplainable family resemblance which sometimes looks out so strangely from faces totally dissimilar. There was a gleam of it now and then; but before you could say, 'It is there,' it had vanished.

By the help of the children, Miss Munroe and I, with the young lady in blue, made occasional spasmodic attempts at conversation; but they always ended abruptly. There are no creatures living more uncompanionable to each other than young ladies who are only slightly acquainted. Mrs Claude, with an amused perception of the state of matters, benevolently came to the rescue. She possessed, in a rare degree, that quick insight which is the highest form of sympathy—itself, I think, one of our Father's good and perfect gifts, which surely we may ask for, if we have it not. Hence her power of making every one about her 'comfortable'—a social talent as uncommon as it is precious.

'Have you read the last number of *Idle Hours*, Miss Munroe?' she asked, taking up a periodical which lay at hand.

'Yes,' said Grace, with a sudden glow over face and neck, which the question seemed by no means to justify.

'How did you like that paper on "Obscure Martyrs?"'

She hesitated a moment, while the crimson glow grew deeper. 'I should think it was written by some one very much in earnest.'

'That paper on "Obscure Martyrs,"' said Mrs Kenway, suddenly breaking in from the other end of the room, where she had caught the subject, '*I* thought it very trashy and superficial—a mere hash, in fact.'

'Two opposite opinions,' said Mrs Claud. 'I should think there is truth in both.'

'How can that be,' asked Miss Kenway, opening her sleepy, blue eyes, with a little stare, 'when they contradict one another so?'

'My dear Lucy,' said her father, 'have you never found out yet that there may be harmony beneath contradiction?'

'Well, in this case, Mrs Claude?' I asked with some curiosity.

'In this case the writer is certainly in earnest, though it is evident she possesses only a limited range of experience, and so she is necessarily superficial.'

'*She!*' said Miss Kenway. 'Why, Mrs Claude, I always thought these papers were by a man. But perhaps you know who wrote them?'

'Indeed, I do not; but it seems to me that the style is thoroughly feminine, both in its strength and its weakness. There are delicate touches here and there that never came from a masculine pen; while I think a man's grasp of the different subjects would be a good deal more comprehensive.'

'Exactly,' said Mr Claude. 'Women never see a thing all round. Their point of view is necessarily limited.'

Grace's eyes shot forth a little indignant flash at this; and Mrs Kenway, I could see, was just about to deliver an elaborate confutation of the heresy, when music was proposed, and the discussion averted.

Grace sat down to the piano, and Ernest, as in duty bound, turned over her music. I almost wondered how she could play, with the gaze of those deep eyes fixed upon her in such undisguised homage. But she seemed as unconscious as a child, and moved and spoke with perfect self-possession.

'Won't you sing?' said Ernest, when she had played a piece or two.

'No; she has a sore throat,' said Mr Claude, mischievously.

Grace laughed, and went on without the usual preface. It was a wild, sweet song she sang, which seemed as if it had never been written, but just welled up fresh from the depths of her own nature. Her voice was a low, thrilling contralto, with a passionate wail in it now and then, which told of many things.

Ernest lingered near her when she had finished, helping her to arrange the music, and giving her every piece upside down, as I could see. He was talking about the article on 'Obscure Martyrs,' which had just been under discussion.

'I could not agree in Mrs Kenway's opinion at all,' he said. 'I thought the paper singularly fresh and original.'

'Did you?' said Grace, with an odd quiver in her voice.

'Yes; didn't you?'

She made no reply for a moment. 'I believe you wrote it yourself,' he remarked, with a keen look at her.

Again the distressful blush; but there was no other answer, except that a shade of annoyance passed over her face. 'Never mind,' said Ernest; 'if you wish this to be a secret, it shall be kept. Won't you trust me?'

'Yes.' And I thought the little monosyllable was spoken with no want of readiness.

I sat long beside my dressing-table that evening, before I could summon courage to disentangle the masses of black hair, which Ernest always liked to see arranged in very complicated braids. How long would he care about it? How soon would my home be broken up a second time?

These and many such questions passed rapidly through my mind. For I could not help seeing that he loved Grace Munroe; and I knew, or thought I knew, what the end would be. For Ernest I could not but rejoice, since I doubted not that he would gain a true-hearted womanly wife, who would set the prose of his life to her own sweet music, and brighten all its dark days with the sunshine of love and trust. But for myself!—it was an hour of weakness, and for a moment sad thoughts overpowered me. How lonely I should be in this wide, wide world! My girlhood was fast passing. My womanhood stretched somewhat drearily before me, very blank, and gray, and still; leading first through the monotonous flats of middle life, and then fading off into a solitary old age.

I suppose such forebodings cast their dark shadow across the mind of every woman, when for the first time she faces the probability that she will have to walk through the world alone. Very foolish they may be; very unbelieving they certainly are; but once in a while they will get the better both of reason and faith. For we do not always stand on the clear mountain heights, whence we can catch the light of our far-off home, and lose sight of all that lies between ; now and then we are down in the valley, where the mist of things present lies upon our spirits like the shadow of death, and shuts out from us the fair land of promise which faith alone makes ours. So it was with me this evening.

I am afraid I wasted nearly an hour in this unprofitable reverie, bringing not only the morrow's burden into the day, but that of my whole future beside, and sinking under it, as well I might. I roused myself at last however, and took up the Bible to read my evening portion. That night my eyes fell first upon the fourth verse of the 47th Psalm : 'He shall choose our inheritance for us.' Often before I had read the words and seen no meaning in them ; but we all know how a truth which, by familiarity and repetition, has become a truism, is kindled afresh into living reality when it is brought home to our present need. We *believed* it before, vaguely, generally ; now we have *faith* in it for ourselves. So it was with the message which came to me to-night. '*He* shall choose.'—my Lord and Master, always wise ; my Father, always loving. Then how should I dare dispute the choice? for even though my heritage might not lie among earth's pleasant places, yet would it not be brightened by His presence who can make even the wilderness rejoice?

Besides, was there not a certain choosing for myself in all this gloomy picturing of the future? How could I tell what my heritage would be? It might be as rich and bright as I fancied it desolate. 'He shall choose,' —not I, with my dim sight and imperfect knowledge. Upon which thought I went to sleep, with a quieter heart, than an hour before I could have supposed possible.

VIII.

UNSATISFIED.

'Thou hast made us for Thyself, O Lord, and our heart is ever unquiet till it finds rest in Thee.'

—St Augustine's *Confessions.*

CHAPTER VIII.

UNSATISFIED.

AND Grace Munroe was an author! I did not like her, as Ernest's future wife, any better for the knowledge of this fact; for the possibility of being both literary and domestic had not been so clearly proved at that time as it is now, and there existed in my mind a necessary, though by no means logical, connection between proof-sheets and confusion.

However, it was not till the following spring that I knew she had written more than an occasional paper in one or two magazines; for her 'nom de plume' effectually concealed her, until a mere accident revealed the young governess as a writer of considerable power and popularity. And here I cannot help breaking off my own story, to record a part of Grace's, which I have heard so often from herself and her brother, that it seems as familiar to me as any incident of my personal history, and I think is likely to be more interesting to any who may hereafter read this chronicle. I will give it in my own words.

The winter had passed, as I have said, and given place to spring sunshine, with its golden promise. The air was everywhere full of a universal soft twitter, even at Everton, where it seemed that the tiny minstrels, who could find no listeners to their domestic idylls among the busy crowds in town, revenged themselves by being specially eloquent in the suburb. They poured a flood of song through the open window of the little sitting-room in Howard Place, where Grace and Kenneth were sitting together one morning, about eleven o'clock; for it was Easter Tuesday, and Grace was released, for a short holiday, from her daily walk to Clayton Square. She was at her desk, her face a little flushed and eager, her hair pushed back, as it always was when she wrote; for it seemed as if the throbbing brow could not even bear this lightest possible pressure.

But her pen was idle now, except that it made a series of dots on the blotting-paper, while its owner leaned back in her chair, and issued domestic orders to Janet, the faithful nurse, Kenneth's foster-mother, who had accompanied them from Scotland, and clung to them through all changing and falling fortunes. She now filled, in her own person, the offices of cook, housemaid, and general care-taker.

The bill of fare for dinner settled, Janet still lingered, fidgeting about the room, under pretence of removing specks of dust, which were invisible to all eyes but her own.

'It's a bonnie mornin', Miss Grace,' she said at length; 'will you and Mr Kenneth no tak' a holiday the day?'

'I haven't time, Janet, thank you,' said Kenneth; 'I must finish this order for Miss Claude's friend.'

'It wad do ye good to get a mouthfu' o' fresh air,' pleaded Janet. 'I'm just vexed to see ye sae white and wan.'

'The air comes to me through the window, Janet,' said Kenneth, 'I needn't go out for it. And, besides, I couldn't walk far enough to get away from houses and pavements.'

So Janet departed, finding she could not carry her point, muttering that somebody's cheeks were like 'twa potatoes.'

And Grace, after she was gone, could not settle to her writing again. There was no denying that Kenneth looked paler and more fragile than ever, and the network of blue veins on his forehead showed with startling distinctness. The long thin fingers moved languidly at their work of wood-carving; and the masses of luxuriant hair were heavy and damp. Grace pushed her chair from the table, and crossed the room to kneel beside his couch.

'Kenneth, darling, you look very tired; do put that stupid work away, and let us have a holiday, as Janet says. Come, my ideas want freshening; let us have an hour's drive.'

But Kenneth shook his head at that, and remarked, oracularly, that 'May-day was coming.'

'Never mind May-day; the rent is nearly ready. Kenneth, I can't bear to see you look so languid and worn-out.'

'It's only the spring, darling;' but he laid his head back wearily, and sighed. 'Sometimes I think it would be very nice if we could have a real holiday, and go somewhere where there was nobody.'

'Rather inconvenient, my dear. I must confess I have no taste for such a Robinson Crusoe expedition.'

'If I could only see the hills once more,' Kenneth continued, without heeding her, 'the grand old hills about Earn, that I remember when I was a child! Oh! Gracie, shall we ever get a sight of Scotland again? You can't think how I dwell upon all the old life there, that was so bright and fresh, before we came to this—this Liverpool.' He broke off abruptly, as if he could not find an adjective to characterise it.

Grace laughed her merry, musical laugh. 'Do you know how often you pull up suddenly in your sentences, when one would expect you were going on for a long time, like a horse at full gallop?'

She was anxious to turn the invalid's thoughts into

another channel; but it was not easily done. He went on murmuring to himself—

> ' "I remember, I remember
> The fir-trees dark and high." '

'Never mind Hood; I'm not in a mood for him. Kenneth, I wonder what those publishers will give me for my story. If I could get £10!'

'Well,—what?'

'Many things; but I was thinking we would go to the sea-side at midsummer.'

'Ah!' said Kenneth, with a sudden sparkle of pleasure, 'how I long for a breath of sea-spray! But we could only go to New Brighton or some of those places; and that muddy Mersey isn't the sea.'

'Don't malign the noble river, Kenneth; half the merchants on 'Change think the Rhine is nothing to him.'

'I wasn't maligning, I was merely stating a fact. But, meantime, the £10 is not forthcoming.'

'No; but I shall surely get something more than compliments. Do you know, Mrs Claude told me yesterday that her husband had actually sat up half the night reading *Thorndale Abbey*, and then lay awake nearly an hour, grumbling that he could see no more of it till next month? Well, I must go on with my transcribing.'

Nevertheless she sat still on the floor by Kenneth's couch, watching the delicate moulding of flowers and fruit as they grew under his knife. While they were in

G

this position, talking of bygone days at Earn, Janet opened the door and ushered in a visitor, a gentleman. Grace gathered herself up from the floor as quickly as she could, upsetting in the process a low stand on which lay Kenneth's tools and blocks, which forthwith flew about the room, as if they had borrowed vitality for the occasion. The stranger smiled, and began to pick up the scattered articles, growing very red-faced over the business, for he was stout and rather elderly.

'Pray, do not give yourself so much trouble,' said Grace, collecting her wits and her gravity, 'we shall easily find them afterwards.'

She glanced meanwhile at the card, which Janet had laid on the table. It bore the name, 'Mr Frederick Rashleigh;' but that told her nothing, so she sat down, as she said afterwards, 'to see what came of it.'

'I am sorry,' said the gentleman, at last subsiding into a chair, and sending out his words in funny little jerks, as if the exertion of stooping had deprived him of breath, 'to have been the occasion of all this confusion; but I was anxious to see Miss Munroe; is she at home?'

Grace looked at Kenneth with quivering lips; but controlled herself to say that she thought she 'had not the pleasure of Mr Rashleigh's acquaintance.'

Miss Munroe! Is it possible? I thought—I beg your pardon—but I expected to see a much older lady. No, we have never met before; but we have had frequent communication by letter. Perhaps I had better introduce myself at once,' he added, smiling, 'as the editor of *Idle Hours.*'

'I'm very glad to see you,' said Grace, rising and extending her hand. But as her vision of an editor had always been of a dried-up looking man, with grizzled hair, and a complexion suggestive of withered oranges, who sat, morning, noon, and night, at a high desk, flanked by huge waste-paper baskets, into which he threw at intervals heaps of unanswered letters, she could not readily transfer her ideas from this mythical personage to the remarkably comfortable reality before her.

'I had a little business in Liverpool,' Mr Rashleigh continued, 'and was glad to give myself the pleasure of calling upon you.' And then, during a desultory talk about the weather and the spring, Grace gradually recovered herself, and she and her unknown correspondent took notes of one another, which were chronicled upon invisible tablets. The small room, the shabby furniture, the invalid on the couch, all came under the stranger's observation, and the conclusions he drew therefrom likewise went down upon the tablets aforesaid.

'You do not ask after *Thorndale Abbey,*' he said at length. 'Is it possible that you are utterly indifferent to its fate?'

'*I* am not, Mr Rashleigh,' answered Kenneth. 'Grace can go on with her writing while you tell me anything there is to tell.'

'Miss Munroe may listen or not as she chooses. I brought some reviews which I will read, if you please.'

He produced a bundle of papers from his pocket, adjusted his spectacles, and peered over them at Grace, who had picked up a piece of knitting, in which she was diligently dropping every other stitch. And then came words of praise, such as she had never dared even to hope for, and predictions of future greatness which dazzled her brain. She looked up, with wondering eyes, to perceive that she had set the novel-reading public in a flame of excitement and expectation, and that, from being an unknown daily governess, she had suddenly stepped into the position of one of the most popular writers of the day.

And still the good man read on and on, long after both his hearers had ceased to heed his words, and were lost in a maze of bewilderment and pleasure. Kenneth, indeed, taught on his couch of pain lessons which his sister had never learned, remembered sadly that the brilliant genius, so highly applauded, brought little honour to Him who had bestowed it. But Grace's delight was as yet unbroken; and she felt, when the reader ceased, as if she were waking from a dream of sweet music. Certainly her knowledge of English commanded no words that would serve her.

'There are two or three more reviews,' continued Mr Rashleigh, with a rather curious expression; 'but you can look at them at your leisure. I should think what

I have read will at least content you ; and I hope the business part of the transaction may be as satisfactory. I have nothing to do with it, properly speaking ; but the publishers requested me to be the bearer of this, and to ask your acceptance of it.'

He placed a roll of notes in her hand, which she looked at with a rather doubtful face ; and then, with a happy perception that his continued presence would be extremely superfluous, took his leave, promising to call again in the evening.

'Oh! Grace,' said Kenneth, when the door was closed, 'how thankful we ought to be!'

He stretched out his arms, and held her in a close embrace. No meed of literary fame, no tribute of praise from a thousand lips, could ever have for Grace the sweetness of that one long kiss. Deep down in her heart's storehouse she treasured it — shrined in memory's fairest setting through many an after year, when the lips that had given it were silent and cold.

But she was not one to let her strongest emotions come readily to the surface ; so she returned it rather shortly, and told him he was a 'silly boy.'

'But oh! Kenneth,' she added, springing up and seizing the notes, which she counted with unsteady fingers, 'we needn't mind May-day now. And you shall have some nice drives, and a sea-trip at midsummer ; and perhaps,' she added, with a comical arching of her eyebrows, 'the authoress of *Thorndale Abbey* may afford to buy a pair of new shoes!'

'What an anti-climax!' laughed Kenneth. And then, in the midst of their merriment, arrived Mrs Claude; and he persisted in telling her all that had happened, while Grace blushed and protested, and pretended to hide her face on his shoulder. And their kind friend's sympathy was so hearty, that one-half the crust of Grace's habitual reserve melted off, and the two drew many steps nearer to each other.

Mrs Claude took them both off for a drive, saying she had brought the carriage for that very purpose. They soon left the town behind, and were out in the open country, where there was little sight or sound of man and man's work. Kenneth, propped up among cushions, drew in fresh draughts of pleasure at every breath. The spring light fell softly everywhere, and glittered far away upon the broad river, of which they caught a glimpse at intervals.

'This beautiful world!' said Kenneth, leaning forward with sparkling eyes. 'Does not nature seem continually striving to convey to us, in her mute figure-speech, some faint shadowing of the glory that is out of sight? And then it is our Father's world, Mrs Claude. How true it is that His children inherit the earth! "All things are yours, and ye are Christ's."'

And Grace listened and sighed. The inheritance was not hers.

In the evening Mr Rashleigh paid his second visit. He urged Grace to promise him another tale, and assured her of liberal remuneration from the publishers; but some undefined feeling prevented her from pledging herself. There was an oppression on her spirits too heavy to be shaken off; and as soon as their visitor had departed, she pleaded the long drive as an excuse for early retiring.

But instead of undressing, she paced her room restlessly for nearly an hour; then extinguished her light, and looked out into the darkness. It was a still, fair night, and the stars shone in a cloudless sky. The Mersey showed like a line of silver in the distance, crossed now and then by some coming or going vessel. Grace watched the dark shadows flitting about with a dreamy, curious interest. They seemed to her morbid fancy to be weaving the thread of her destiny, while she could only look on, without power to touch or change. She pressed her forehead against the cool glass, as if to still its feverish throbbing. Then she paced the room again; but with lighter steps now, lest she should disturb the sleeper in the next room.

It had come at last—the fame she had often pictured, sometimes thirsted for; and it had brought with it what, to the sister's heart, was more precious than all beside— added comforts for the cherished sufferer, who was, in truth, her 'other dearer life in life.' And yet any one who had seen the drooping figure and weary face, would

not have thought them very appropriate for the successful authoress, whose name was on so many lips.
Poor Grace! How many, like her, have turned aside
with bitterness from the mocking shadow which they
had mistaken for substance!

Then some flattering sentences from the reviews she
had just heard rang on her ears again, and for a moment
her heart beat proudly at the meed of well-earned
praise. 'But it isn't enough; it doesn't satisfy me,' she
murmured. 'I would give it all up to have some one to
take care of me—some love strong enough to lean upon
and rest in, different even from Kenneth's. Oh! mother,
mother!' she added, passionately, looking up into the
blue, star-lit sky, 'I am so weary and lonely. All these
voices that are ringing outside never reach my heart.
There is such a terrible silence there, I cannot bear it?'
and she bent her head in an agony and moaned aloud.
What was fame to her now?

Other thoughts followed, even more bitter. One or
two of the reviews which Mr Rashleigh had left for her
perusal had been a little ironical and severe; and a flush
of distress and mortification mounted to her cheeks as
she thought of them. It was bad enough to be reviewed
at all—to have the confidences bestowed upon that
mythical 'public' examined and anatomized by actual
editors—dry, disagreeable men, as her imagination still
pictured them, in spite of that day's experience to the
contrary. She would have needed a single eye and a

pure motive to sustain her even against this. But to be criticised and found fault with; accused now of one mistake or blemish, and now of its very opposite,—here was something far worse, something from which her shy, shrinking reticence recoiled with exceeding pain. And what was it for, after all? Why had she exposed herself to these shafts of criticism? exchanged the safe shelter of her quiet home-life for this terrible publicity? Why? —oh, why?

Every woman who writes must expect to be harassed by such questions; and it is well for her if her answer is ready at hand in the honest conviction that she has simply fulfilled the work given, delivered the message committed to her, spoken out of the felt need of her own heart to meet the need of another, or cast upon the broad waters of human thought some little seed of truth, which shall surely be found.

But poor Grace was without any such comfort. Of the thousands of readers whom her pages held entranced and breathless, not one was likely to rise from their perusal with a truer and more healthy view of life, with higher aims and nobler purposes. The royal stamp of genius was upon the book, but it was genius unconsecrated; and now, in the silent hours, when the soul comes face to face with realities, Grace felt this, and owned it with shame and sorrow. There were thorns hidden among the laurel leaves, and the crowned brow was wounded and bleeding.

However, she settled into her ordinary life again; received, with great composure, Mr Claude's congratulations when his wife told him 'the news of the day,' as he smilingly said; and heard her pupils blunder through Latin rules and French verbs, as if she had never done anything else.

But one day, as she was coming home from town, tripping along in the gray cloak and cottage bonnet, which was her usual out-door trim, she met Mr Kenway. She would have bowed and passed on, for he was scarcely more than a stranger, though they had spent several evenings together at Mrs Claude's; but he was crossing the street, and she was obliged to stop.

'I have only just learned,' he said, smiling, 'that "May Blossom" is a flower of our own growing.'

'Nay,' said Grace, with a quick flush of colour, 'it has only been transplanted from northern hills.'

'Ah! well, it has taken kindly root, and must be naturalized by this time.' He was walking on beside her, and Grace counted the pavement in an uncomfortable wonder what she should say next.

'You have a great talent entrusted to your keeping, Miss Munroe,' pursued her companion.

'I wish I hadn't,' said Grace, with a little tremulous abruptness in her voice, which betrayed a world of unrest within.

'Why?' The grave eyes were bent upon her with a look of keen inquiry; but she did not answer it.

'Certainly the power of influencing so many minds, of raising echoes which shall vibrate through all time, and on into eternity, *is* very terrible. I do not wonder that you feel the possession of it an almost overwhelming responsibility.'

'I never realised it till now,' said Grace, in tones which he could barely hear. 'If I had only thought of it before!'

'Then, perhaps,' said her listener, with a curious smile, 'in the light of this new idea, the applause you have earned hardly satisfies you.'

Grace shook her head, with a long sigh. Mr Kenway was silent a few minutes; and when at length he spoke, it was to call away her thoughts from herself, and fix them on another.

'I was much struck this morning with those words one has heard a thousand times, and yet they are always sweet and fresh, "Come unto me, all ye that labour and are heavy laden, and I will give you rest." *There* is a promise of something that will satisfy.'

'Yes, I know,' said Grace, breaking in with her accustomed formula.

'I am sure you *know*, my dear young lady; but this is not a question of knowing, but of *feeling*. Christianity is a life, not a doctrine.'

He said no more till they had climbed the hill, and stood at the door of Grace's home, which nestled close under Everton Church.

'No, I must not stay,' he said then, in answer to her

request ; 'and I must ask you to forgive me, if I have said what has given you pain.'

'Oh no,' said Grace eagerly ; 'I do need that rest, Mr Kenway, and I cannot find it.'

'I will give you Christ's words—they are better help than mine—"*Come unto me ;*" and this, a prayer which has guided me through many a difficulty, "Oh send forth thy light and thy truth, let them lead me."' He shook hands warmly and was gone.

That walk was a memorable one for the young authoress. It witnessed the first dawn of light upon her spiritual horizon—light which brightened indeed but slowly, and was obscured by many a cloud, but which should know no setting henceforth, here or hereafter. The peculiar cast of her mind, partly speculative, partly sceptical, occasioned her many difficulties, and Kenneth's simplicity was sometimes sorely perplexed by her questionings, which would indeed have scandalized many, too shallow or too indifferent to be anything but orthodox. In fact, her determination to think out everything for herself, led her into depths where the only standing ground was one which her pride rebelled against—a simple acceptance of 'Thus saith the Scripture.' She would not acknowledge that joy and peace could come to her only 'in believing ;' that speculative difficulties must often be left without explanation ; that 'faith, in fact, *is* faith, and not demonstration.'*

---

* Goodwin's *University Sermons.*

On the other hand, her sympathy with everything which seemed to her proscribed or persecuted, tempted her to embrace sundry conflicting opinions at one and the same moment, simply because they were those of a minority branded by others as unsound.

'What can I do,' she said, impatiently, to Kenneth one day, 'cooped up in this narrow evangelicism, with its bitterness and intolerance?'

She was walking up and down, the little nervous fingers working as if they struggled with material bolts and bars. Kenneth looked up in amaze at this outburst, to which his wits could frame no immediate reply.

'Hadn't you better let all the *izms* alone for the present?' he said at length. 'It seems to me that we have neither of us got beyond this, "Lord, what wilt Thou have *me* to do?"'

'*I* haven't,' said Grace, more gently; 'but still, these things vex me, Kenneth.'

'They are human nature, dear, not evangelicism.'

'Yes; one certainly need not go far to find them. I'm afraid I have shown small charity in my very condemnation of the want of it.'

Still, in spite of these wilful interludes, Grace held fast the clue which had been put into her hands. And her prayer to be taught that which she could not see, was answered by discoveries which left her little time to criticise the shortcomings of others, whether parties or persons. The sense of personal need, the consciousness of personal guilt, grew daily stronger within, and lighted up for her, with new and terrible meaning, many phrases which she had hitherto wondered at and scorned. She felt that her whole past life, notwithstanding its apparent sacrifice, had nevertheless been a worship of self, and that the gifts which God's hand had bestowed, had occupied the throne of the Giver. She saw how her darkness needed the light of God's Spirit, and her ignorance the teaching of His truth; how for her, the brilliant child of genius, as for the meanest household drudge, there was but one way of pardon and acceptance—through the blood of the Lamb that was slain.

It was long, indeed, before this confession was wrung from her reluctant lips; long before pride would submit to what reason and feeling acknowledged.

'There are so many questions,' she said one day to Mr Kenway.

'So many,' was the quiet reply, '*if we will ask them.* But the spirit of questioning is not the spirit of a child; and yet Jesus said, "Except ye become as little children." And besides, if the one central question is settled, it throws light on all the rest. Or if they remain still dark and dim, they need not shake our faith.'

They were sitting together in the little parlour at Howard Place. It was Saturday afternoon; Mrs Claude had taken Kenneth for a drive, but Grace preferred remaining at home to write. So, at least, she said; but the pen drooped idly between her fingers, and, with her head bent upon her hand, she was lost in a long fit of troubled musing, when Janet announced Mr Kenway.

Grace welcomed him eagerly; and soon, almost unconsciously to herself, he had drawn from her some of the thoughts which his arrival had interrupted. He found her, however, a little disposed to wander over a very wide field of controversy, and his last remark had been intended to bring her home again. A sigh was Grace's only answer to it, until at last, with a sudden contradictory impulse, she looked up and said—

'You speak, Mr Kenway, as if you were quite sure that there is a central question to be settled?'

'Yes, I am sure,' he answered with a smile; 'so are you.'

'I don't know,' said Grace sadly; 'sometimes I could doubt everything. Things invisible, and often things visible too, are like the misty, shadowy shapes that one sees in a dream. Or else if I feel that *they* are real, then there is a kind of numbness upon myself, and I cannot grasp them.'

'Ah! that is it—the numbness *is* upon yourself. Have you prayed that it might be taken away?'

'Yes,' said Grace, rather hesitatingly; 'but how could I, Mr Kenway, when I was not sure whether it was of any use?'

He smiled. 'Will you promise me to leave that question aside for a little? *Will you pray earnestly, perseveringly;* and if you cannot believe, will you ask that your unbelief may be helped? The man with the withered hand had no strength to stretch it out at the command of Christ; but *he stretched it out*, and it was "restored whole as the other." Power came with obedience. And so with your difficulty about prayer. *By praying*, you will find it solved.'

'I began a course of reading on the evidences of Christianity,' said Grace; 'but it didn't help me much.'

'Most likely not. We thank God, indeed, that the foundations of our belief are laid deep in historic fact; that its records abide the severest test of criticism, and prove themselves to be no cunningly devised fables, but words of truth and soberness. But still, the faith by which our souls *live*, is not to be won thus. Its best evidence is the sense of our own need—the need which none but Christ can fill; the deep wound within—the plague there, which none but He can heal. Ask God to show you more of that; and remember that what is dark to the intellect, becomes clear to the heart.* Forgive me,' he added, as if recollecting himself; 'I have spoken perhaps too plainly.'

'Oh no, no,' said Grace eagerly; 'you do not know how I have longed for some one to guide me in these things.'

'I should be so thankful if I could be of the least use to you, Miss Munroe; but, after all, I think we get the

---

* 'L'Ecriture sainte n'est pas une science de l'esprit mais du cœur.'— PASCAL, *Pensées*.

truest help by simply waiting upon God. "He that followeth me shall not walk in darkness, but shall have the light of life." That is one of those deep words of our Lord which He only has treasured up for us who leaned upon His breast—the beloved disciple who shared most fully the spirit of his Master. It is a *sure* word, spoken by the faithful and *true* Witness. And you see to whom the promise is given : to him "that followeth ;" not to those who will not submit to what they cannot see, who will not "cease from their own wisdom," or believe that to simplicity, faith, and prayer, are revealed things hidden from distrust and pride,—not to any of these is the light given ; for of them it is rather true that when it shineth in darkness, the darkness comprehendeth it not ; but to him that followeth. "If any man will do"—is *willing* to do—"his will, he shall know of the doctrine."'

If these last words implied a measure of rebuke, it was so gently administered that Grace could not feel offended.

'Thank you, Mr Kenway,' she answered meekly, 'I will try to think of what you say.'

But now there was a sound of wheels at the door, and she sprang up to help Kenneth from the carriage. Only as her visitor took leave, he repeated gently—

'Remember ; *him that followeth.*'

Grace sat by the sitting-room fire that night after

H

Kenneth had been asleep for hours.   She thought over all that Mr Kenway had said, and recalled especially the parting injunction, which reminded her of another and a higher Teacher.

Almost mechanically she took up her Bible to read the words for herself; but such a rush of associations came over her, as she turned the leaves to find that fourth Gospel from which he had quoted, that for a few minutes she was fain to lay it down again, to prevent them from being blotted by tears.

She remembered how, long years ago, she had sat on her mother's knee to read, for the first time, a few words out of that Holy Book, which many 'sweet stories of old' had already taught her to love.   From this very Gospel she had read, in the first chapter, while her mother's finger traced out the lines ; and she could recall, even now, the difficulty of that long word 'comprehended' in the fifth verse, and the simple, loving explanation which followed, from lips which in 'dear words of human speech,' would open now no more.

And then memory took up another link, and she saw herself again a child, kneeling to repeat the evening prayer which those same silent lips had taught : ' Lighten our darkness, we beseech Thee, O Lord ; and by Thy great mercy defend us from all perils and dangers of this night, for the love of Thine only Son, our Saviour Jesus Christ.   Amen.'

Ah ! was it not needed still ?   Was there not a darkness deeper far than that outward one on which her infant thoughts had rested? Were there no 'perils and dangers' in that night of the soul, which seemed now to envelope her so closely, so hopelessly? Should not the prayer of her infancy be the prayer of maturer years? Should it not rather be the prayer of her life; its need never outgrown; but rather every day more truly realized?

And so she knelt and prayed once more, with deeper meaning though with weaker faith: 'Lighten my darkness, I beseech Thee, O Lord, open Thou mine eyes, that I may see the Light of Life.'

Long after midnight, Grace was still turning over the pages of that Gospel of the beloved disciple—that Gospel which gives us, not a summary of doctrines, but the record of Life which is the source of life; not a system of morality, but the living, loving, portraiture of the 'Word made flesh.' And as she read the holy narrative—so calm and yet so graphic, so simple and yet so full of power, with the seal of perfect fidelity in each detail—'he that *saw it* bare record, and we *know* that his record is true,'—her doubts seemed to vanish one by one, like mists before the sun, and she bowed her head in meek submission to the noble confession with which the story closes: 'These are written, that ye might believe that Jesus is the Christ, the Son of God; and that believing ye might have life through his name.'

IX.

OUTWARD AND INWARD.

'The tears that in life's wondrous alchemy
Work change, that change of very being seems.'

Isa Craig.

CHAPTER IX.

OUTWARD AND INWARD.

I SOON heard from Mrs Claude the story of Grace's literary fame, which, as I have said, did not greatly incline me to welcome her as Ernest's future wife. And when, as was frequently the case now, I spent my evenings alone, while he, upon one pretext or other, yielded to the attraction which drew him from the straight road from Liverpool to Wavertree up to the top of Everton Hill; my thoughts were apt to wander from the marriage settlement or mortgage deed I might be engrossing, into dreams of the future, which were not tinted with rose, either for him or for myself.

Yet I was obliged to confess that, in all I had seen of Grace (and our intimacy was now tolerably familiar), I had never been able to discover the slightest stain of ink on the small fingers which were generally busied in some purely feminine occupation. Indeed, I had seen these same fingers execute marvels of neat stitchery, which left my own performances in that line entirely in the shade. But still I could not quite forgive them for having meddled with pens and paper. Sisters are proverbially jealous of a brother's matrimonial choice; and, I suppose it would have been hard to convince me that any woman living was good enough for Ernest.

I was sitting at my desk one warm evening in early June, thinking of this among other matters, and allowing my pen frequent pauses as I did so. Indeed, it was almost too hot to write; the day had been sultry and close; the sun unveiled by a single pitiful cloud; the air perfectly still, except for an occasional scorching breath, which seemed to come from the very mouth of a furnace. The white pavements shimmered through the heat, and foot-passengers, even the most business-like, walked with a lagging step, looking as if they would not walk at all if they could help it. Cab and omnibus horses gasped wearily along, whips, for the most part, hanging mercifully motionless in the drivers' hands, for it would have been too much trouble to use them.

I had spent the greater part of the day on the sofa, struggling with fever and weariness which I could not throw off; but now, towards seven o'clock, I roused myself to finish some work which I knew would be needed on the morrow. Surely Ernest could not be long! I listened, with more than usual impatience, for the sound of the omnibus drawing up at the gate, which would be followed, I knew, by the springing step on the gravel, and the turning of the key in the latch. But omnibus after omnibus passed without slackening speed: it was no use waiting longer; I must order tea, and drink it alone. But, if he has climbed Everton Hill in all this heat, things must be nearing a crisis!

However, I had not finished my solitary meal before he came, looking jaded and worn, and withal, as I thought, a little out of temper. What could be the matter? It was on my lips to ask; but I fortunately checked the words before they passed further.

Nothing annoys a man more than to be eagerly questioned when he comes home tired. Give him a neatly-served dinner, or a pair of easy slippers and a cup of tea, and let him eat and drink in peace, and in time he will tell you, of his own proper motion, all you wish to know. But if you begin the attack too soon, the chances are that you will be rewarded by curtly spoken monosyllables. Put down that piece of wisdom in your note-book, girls; it will serve you well some day.

My patience on this particular occasion was somewhat tried. Tea passed almost in silence; so did half an hour which Ernest spent in moody pacings up and down, stopping now and then to pick off and pull to pieces some unoffending flowers, which stood in a small vase on my desk. Their sweet breath and gentle teaching had refreshed me through many hours of that weary day, and it was rather hard to see the bright rose leaves strewing the floor; but, after all, they only shared the fate of other more precious things which are crushed by an unthinking touch.

At length, I ventured to ask very gently if anything had happened to disturb him. Still no answer; but this time a hassock was kicked from one side of the room to the other. I went up to him now, and laid my hand with the lightest possible touch upon his arm. He stopped, and took it fast in his, saying, in a voice which sounded strangely hollow and sad, 'Elsie, I've made a fool of myself to-day.'

'I don't believe it.'

'Yes, I have. I proposed to Grace Munroe, and was rejected.'

'Rejected!' If Grace had stood in my way at that moment, there might have been danger of assault and battery.

'Yes—it's a new sensation—not altogether a pleasant one.' He laughed—a bitter laugh, which made me shiver,—and then we walked without a word for nearly an hour. These crises in life are not the times for talking. Even the readiest tongues are constrained to yield now and then to the force of silence.

'Does she love any one else, Ernest?' I asked.

'No; that I am sure of. And the strangest part of it is that I believe she loves me. "Two or three months ago it might have been," she said; "but not

now." You women are such incomprehensible creatures.'

I looked up with a long breath of relief. Then, at
least, she was no coquette; and, if she truly cared for
Ernest, she would not thoughtlessly trifle with his love.

'We must trust her, Ernest. If she is worthy to be
loved at all, she is worth that. But did she give you no
reason ?'

'Yes; only I don't see the force of it in the least.
And she made me promise to tell no one, not even you.'

Certainly it did seem perplexing, and in my secret
heart I could not help feeling a little angry. Still I
could only plead, with Ernest and with myself, 'Let us
have faith in one another.'

'I'll tell you how it was, Elsie,' said my brother,
throwing himself on the sofa, and drawing me to rest
beside him. 'I went up to Everton to see Kenneth, who
has been very poorly since last Monday, for I know the
days are long and dreary for him when he is not able to
amuse himself with his carving. And he told me—for
he trusts me now as if I were his brother—that Grace
had been dismissed from Mrs Herbert's. She goes
there, you know, three afternoons in the week, to teach
those precious children, whom their devoted mother con-
siders in the light of stray angels. It's curious to see a
gentle, passive nature like Kenneth's once thoroughly
roused and stirred. I didn't think there had been so
much passion in the boy; but certainly Mrs Herbert's

treatment of Grace was enough to rouse any fellow's indignation. She came into the schoolroom, when the children were there, and told Grace, in their presence, that her system of teaching was defective, and that she might consider herself at liberty to form another engagement as soon as she chose—"her pupils were not making satisfactory progress." She forgets, as Kenneth said, that there isn't a single element of progress in them. However, Grace would not have cared anything about it, if Mrs Herbert had treated her courteously, as one lady ought to treat another; and if she judged her fit to be the educator of her children, she has surely some claim to the title. I shall never respect Mrs Herbert from this time.'

'It was very inconsiderate, certainly.'

'Inconsiderate, Elsie! It was wrong—heartless. And she calls herself a Christian,' Ernest went on, his blue eyes flashing with an angry light, 'and preaches about worldly conformity! I wonder which is the greater sin, straining at a gnat or swallowing a camel!'

'These ought ye to have done, and not have left the other undone.'

'Yes, yes, I know, Elsie; but I do get so weary of this stale, worn-out modern Christianity, with its abundant profession for those that are outside, and its wonderfully hollow practice for all that look behind the scenes. I tell you, Elsie, there is not half the honour, and high principle, and courteous delicacy of feeling among your religious friends, that there is among those who don't profess to be anything but what they are.'

Poor Ernest! He was always specially keen-sighted for the inconsistencies of those whom he called 'good' people, by way of quieting an uneasy consciousness, that his own goodness was rather equivocal. I had always welcomed this antagonism as a healthy sign. It was, at least, an evidence of life. But what could I say in reply? Alas, alas! for the 'stones of stumbling' cast in the narrow way by those who profess to love and follow it!

'I'm afraid it's all too true, Ernest. But surely we are not to take our Christianity from Christians, but from Christ.'

'Christians!' echoed Ernest, catching one word of my answer, and heedless of the rest; 'isn't it a desecration of the name? If they were more patient, and self-sacrificing, and forbearing, and considerate than other people, I could believe in it. But it's all sham and unreality.'

One half the bitterness of this tirade was due, I knew, to the excited feeling of the moment; but still it sadly reminded me that, on one subject—the dearest and most sacred of all—our thoughts and hopes were not agreed; and in a moment the idea struck me, could it be this which had come between him and Grace? But of course I could ask nothing, and Ernest went back to the story of the afternoon.

'You will wonder what all this has to do with what I told you before. Well, the truth is, I met Grace as I was coming home, and I couldn't help telling her how sorry I felt for all her troubles, and how gladly I would shield her from them if she would let me. In short, as I said, I made a fool of myself. How mad I was not to wait longer!'

And where was Grace at this time! Alone in her room,—alone with her agony. Not weeping; hers was no grief to find relief in tears, but murmuring with white lips—

'My Saviour, I do this for Thee.'

The next few weeks are a mere blank in my memory; for, before another night, I was attacked by a low nervous fever, brought on by sitting too closely at my desk, which kept me prostrate for many days.

Very dreary days they were. Our kind landlady tended me with unfailing care and patience; but she was not born to be a nurse, and her very zeal and eagerness defeated their object. She could not enter the room without bringing into it that indescribable *bustle* so intensely irritating to the sick; and she used to ask me so often if I wanted anything, that I was sorely tempted to reply, 'Yes, I should be glad if you would let me alone.' No one knows the misery of being tended in illness by persons who have no 'sick sensations' themselves, or have forgotten them, if they ever had; who will read you, for amusement, a list of crimes and casualities from a crackling newspaper; or, by way of being very quiet, will speak in the loud whisper which almost makes you scream.

There was another trouble too, in which neither Mrs Smith nor Ernest could help me. Like many persons to whom illness has been much a matter of theory—for, from childhood upwards, my health had been almost unbroken—I had accustomed myself to think of it as a kind of sanctuary, in which, shut out from the cares and temptations of life, one could grow 'good' as a matter of necessity. I had expected to feel God always near—to be still in His presence, like a quiet lake, reflecting His peace, and bright with His praise.

But I found, on the contrary, that many hours passed away in the mere endurance of pain, or of that absolute weakness which is in itself suffering; and that there were many more in which my mind was an entire blank, incapable of thought, or even of recollection. I used to fancy it went away altogether now and then, leaving me with a mere body—a bundle of sensations, nothing more. All which was very confusing and disappointing, and, at the time, occasioned me no small disquiet, though afterwards I came to see that, even in these waste places, God's hand had been with me when I knew it not, teaching me unconscious lessons which I hardly seemed to learn, and strengthening the life of the spirit even through physical pain and oppression.

And surely such seasons render more precious than ever that high-priestly office of our Lord, which links

Him in such tender sympathy with our human weakness and want! For He fails not to gather up the broken fragments of our prayers—all unuttered though they may be—and to present them, a pure offering, before His Father and ours. And when prayer, and even thought, seem impossible, submission and silence may still be an acceptable sacrifice in His sight, who 'knoweth all our desire,' and from whom even our 'groaning' is not hid.

Ernest was an excellent nurse, joining to his manly strength the tact and tenderness of a woman—at least, of some women; for I have known feminine fingers that were both rough and awkward. And I think it was good for him to have his thoughts in some measure diverted and occupied by his attendance upon me, though his grave, wearied look often went to my heart, and I knew well that one secret care was with him always. I could do nothing to help him. I could only pray that God might be with him in the strife, and lead him through its very agony to the one true source of healing.

It is very sad to watch our loved ones pass into the cloud whither we cannot follow, and drink the cup of trembling we may not share. But what rest, what comfort, are in the knowledge that we may bring our sorrow and tenderness to One who loves them better than we, and ask Him to take care of the precious things which our weak hands are powerless to shield!

My strength returned very slowly. The long summer days were spent on the sofa, and the nights in a terror of nervous fears, which would not be put down by either reason or ridicule. I began to wonder what would be the end of it—whether I should ever feel the thrill of health again, or whether my life would waste gradually away, mind and body alike crumbling in a slow but sure decay.

However, the tonic I needed was at hand. One morning, on entering the sitting-room after Ernest had left for town, I found on the table a letter, bearing the Greyslope postmark, which I knew at once was from Mary Wilton. Her letters were very few, for she was much occupied; but they were always welcome when they came, and to-day I broke the seal with more than usual eagerness, glad of even the smallest break in the monotony of invalid life. And the first page contained an invitation to Greyslope: 'Papa thinks your native air will probably be the best medicine. So come, dear Elsie, as soon as you are able to travel, and let me try my powers of nursing. You will not refuse, I know.'

No fear of that! Already the very thought seemed to have brought strength with it. The breath of the hills would cool the fever on my brain better than any-thing else. I lay back on the sofa, giving myself up to the fair vision which fancy touched with such vivid colouring; and half an hour passed before I could rouse myself to finish Mary's closely-written pages. And I

I

was not a little startled to find in one of them a reference to a subject she had never touched upon before.

'I wonder whether I shall find you much changed, Elsie,' she wrote (since she seemed to take for granted that her invitation would be accepted). 'I almost fancy not; for your letters show me your old self in full force and freshness. For myself, I sometimes wonder whether the Mary of the present and the Mary of those former days can be the same. I was very wretched when you left Heatherstone, Elsie—very wretched and very proud. Life seemed strangely dark and empty. I was striving to bury the past in a shroud of tender memories, and to fasten it down with a stern resolve, striving to bear my burden alone, and closing my heart against all comfort, either human or divine. Often, often I wondered whether that long agony would ever end. But it passed away in God's good time, when I came at last to Him for sym- pathy,—not strong, as I had fancied, or even patient, as I had striven to make myself, but only weary, and help- less, and sad. And then He comforted me! Not all at once, nor by a miracle, steeping my soul in Lethe, but gradually, almost imperceptibly, so revealing to me by His Spirit the things of Christ, that the spell which was upon me has lost its deeper power. I have not got back my childhood's heart again, nor ever gained that "slumber deep," in which my dream might be as though it had not been. In the quietest sleep the dream will return ; but I do not struggle now to cast it entirely aside. I take it rather afresh to the Lord, who has taught me the truth of His own word : " He hath torn, and he will heal ; He hath smitten, and he will bind up."

'When you come we will not touch upon this ; but I was anxious to say thus much by letter.'

And then the letter concluded, though it was followed by the inevitable postcript : 'Come as soon as you can, Elsie ; for I am not sure whether we can accommodate you later in the autumn, as there is to be a family migration to the seaside. Edward Grey may be with us during a part of your visit; but you will not mind that.'

Certainly not. Why should I ?

Edward Grey was an orphan ward of Dr Wilton's, whom I remembered dimly as a boy, though my only distinct recollection of him was as an Oxford graduate, down at Greyslope for 'the long.' On one of these occasions he had driven over to Heatherstone with Dr Wilton, who wished to see my father upon business. Aunt Margaret was out, and I, at home for my midsummer holidays, was left to entertain Mr Grey in the dining-room, while the two gentlemen consulted in the study.

Being much at a loss for something to say, and remembering that my visitor was fond of music, I opened the jingling square piano, which stood in a corner of the room, and asked if he would play me a tune, by which means I hoped to secure both his amusement and my own.

'Oh yes, love,' answered the great man, bestowing upon me a patronising smile. 'What shall I play?'

'Anything you like,' I answered, shortly. It was too much. What business had he to call me 'love?'—me, a young lady, and not a mere chit, as he seemed to suppose!

My lips were parted for an indignant protest; but a certain instinct warned me that it would be more dignified to keep silence.

And from that day to this I had never seen Edward Grey; nor, if the truth must be told, had I ever entirely forgiven him.

X.

A PILGRIMAGE TO OLD SHRINES.

''Tis now become a story little known,
That once we called the pastoral house our own.'

COWPER.

CHAPTER X.

A PILGRIMAGE TO OLD SHRINES.

O H the joy of breathing once more the air of my beloved north! The delight of seeing the hills again, with their glorious lights and shadows, and the calm of their peaceful strength!

I believe my eyes were rather misty when I caught the first glimse of them, for there rose suddenly from the treasured past a strong yearning for the 'touch of a vanished hand, and the sound of a voice that is still.' Yet I could thank God heartily for opening to me once more the gorgeous treasure-chambers of this His beautiful world, and permitting me to gaze again in silent wonder and delight upon the noble works of His hand!

Ernest and I—for, in my weakness, he would not hear of my travelling alone—reached Greyslope in the evening, in time for tea, that most social of all meals, which possesses so wonderful a power of charming away the stiffness that *will* gather insensibly, even over true friends, when they meet for the first time after long separation. How doubly pleasant that tea-table was, with its hospitable north country cheer, and the genial welcome which was worth far more!

There were many threads of silver now in Dr Wilton's hair, and some snowy lines among his wife's curls; but in other respects time seemed to have touched them lightly. *He* looked, I thought, less grave and anxious, altogether less professional than I had formerly known him; and the good lady was full as ever of bustle and kindness, keeping up the same perpetual ripple of talk, which I always thought must account for her husband's taciturnity.

And Mary! Time had brought her nothing but good. I could see that, even by an imperfect glimpse of her as she sat behind the urn to pour out tea. She looked even younger than when we parted, for her brow had grown more placid, and the lines of habitual self-command had a little relaxed their strain. Her eyes, that used to look drearily out on life, as if they saw it all 'equal in one snow,' were shining now with the quiet light which tells of a heart at rest.

And while we lingered in our chat, its occasional pauses filled up by the soft clink of silver and china, the door opened and admitted an addition to our party, in the shape of a figure in easy clerical undress, who was greeted by Mrs Wilton with—

'Well, Edward, I hope you've tired yourself to your satisfaction?'

Of course this was Mr Grey. He shook hands, with the original remark, that he had the pleasure of meeting Miss Ellis before ; and then addressed himself to some potted trout, as if they were for the present a greater attraction.

'Edward has had a long walk,' explained Mrs Wilton. She called him 'Edward' still—good, motherly woman— in spite of his white tie.

'One of a series,' added that gentleman. 'I am exploring the neighbourhood systematically.' Which I was glad to hear, and hoped the series would last during my stay at Greyslope. Somehow I did not fancy Mr Grey.

The next day Ernest and I drove over to Heatherstone,—in silence for the most part, since thought and memory were alike too busy for speech ; except that once Ernest recurred to a subject which had not been named since that memorable evening at Wavertree, and told me that, the day before he left home, he had met Grace Munroe in the street, looking very pale, and as if she too were suffering.

'I can't understand it in the least,' he added. 'Why should she persist in spoiling both my life and her own for the sake of an idea?'

'I don't ask to be told what the idea is, Ernest,' I

replied, 'though I can't help guessing it. But I am very sure that Grace will not do this thing lightly.'

Ernest said no more, and I could only, as I had often done before,

> 'Leave it all in His high hand
> Who doth hearts, as streams, command.'

We called at the parsonage, and received a most cordial welcome; though my dear father's successor, who reminded me of a kindly, good-tempered bear, was about as unlike him as one man could be unlike another. There was an odour of stale tobacco in the bachelor-looking den which was once our pretty drawing-room, and on the window seat where my fuschias had flourished, was a pile of books that looked as if they had neither been opened nor dusted for years.

But it was the old house still, and there were spirit-voices calling me from every nook and corner of it, though I hardly dared listen to them, lest they should bring tears I might not spare time to shed. However, our rough host showed a touch of delicate feeling for which I was not prepared, for he gave Ernest the key of the Church, and told us to go there alone; he knew we should like it better.

And so we trod once more the little well-worn path, and stood by our parent's grave. Everything was very still. No stir of busy life around to break upon the silence of death. Nature's voice, indeed, was not silent;

but that seldom jars upon us in any mood. And it even seemed as if the afternoon light fell more softly upon the grey stone, with its simple lettering, which marked the spot where our dead were at rest. And yet they were not there! We know little of the blessed spirits who have 'departed hence in the Lord.' We cannot penetrate what God has sealed in silence. Our words are too weak, our ears too dull, our hearts too earthly, to learn the mysteries which He has not revealed ; but one thing we do surely know, that they are 'with Christ, which is far better ;' and so we who walk in His light during our waiting time on earth, may look up with hope from the grave whither we go to weep, and feel that we are still one with those who are at rest.

On our return to Greyslope, we called at Ivyburn. Miss Melville was in her old trim—gardening gloves and bonnet, the latter of a fashion which no bonnet but hers ever knew. She was a trifle less erect, perhaps, than formerly, but not one whit less bright and fresh. There are some who never grow old. Do we not all know them, and have we not rejoiced in their quaint, innocent fun, and gleeful laugh, which retains to the end the clear ring of childhood? The sunshine of the earlier year lingers on through all the frosts of the later. The passion-flowers have faded, but the Christmas wreath has a glory of its own.

'You must not think of remaining at Greyslope all the while you are in the north, Elsie,' said Miss Melville, as we prepared to drive home. 'My child, you have lived among town smoke till you have grown thin upon it. You must come here to drink milk, and be fattened.'

So it was arranged. And the following day Ernest returned to Liverpool.

XI.

TALKS BY TWILIGHT AND SUNLIGHT.

'Then, as they talked, they touched on solemn things,
  As ever human talk will touch
  When hearts are open.'

ISA CRAIG.

CHAPTER XI.

TALKS BY TWILIGHT AND SUNLIGHT.

IT was Sabbath evening, the second after my arrival at Greyslope. The services of the day were over, being held morning and afternoon, as is often the case in country districts, and had been at Greyslope from time immemorial; for its inhabitants, who were as conservative in habit as they were radical in politics, would have thought the times were seriously out of joint if they had been summoned to Church in an evening.

I had retreated to my room for an hour's quiet, glad to escape for a time from the somewhat noisy party, whose fulness of life and spirit was rather overwhelming to my still unsteady nerves, and glad, too, to bring into the presence of my heavenly Father some restless thoughts which had been unmanageable during the day.

This family group made me feel a little lonely; for

in all the wide world I had 'none to love me best.' No father's hand rested tenderly on my brow. No mother's voice soothed me with its soft music. A sister's love I had never known, and in Ernest's heart I knew that I held no longer the first place. The old weakness came over me, and I sat looking out upon the wide landscape, lying fair in its Sabbath rest, until it was blotted from my sight by tears.

A low knock at the door, and I heard Mary's voice asking admittance.

'I came to see if you were ill, Elsie,' she said. 'Papa noticed you were looking very pale.'

'Not ill, only tired,' I answered, as steadily as I could; but I think my voice must have betrayed me, for she bent over me with a wistful look.

'May I stay with you a little, Elsie? We have been looking at one another through a mist ever since you came, and I don't think it will clear off till we have one of our old talks.'

But we did not talk even now. We sat in silence, in which there is sometimes truer communion than in speech. At last Mary said, observant, I think, of my heavy eyes—

'Sabbath evenings are always rather sad times, are they not?—full of a kind of yearning loneliness, made up of thoughts which dwell too much both on the past and the future. The *near* future, I mean,' she added; 'for oh, Elsie, if we could only keep our minds fixed on the *distant* future—"the rest that remaineth!" And the near future will soon be the past. How blessed it is to think of that! How little it matters about the ups and downs that lie between, if we only take the right road, and get home at last!'

'Yes; but our hold of these things is weak at the best, Mary, and sometimes they seem to slip from our grasp altogether.'

'Ah! yes; but they are *real* still, whether we grasp them or not; and it is such a comfort to turn from the weakness of feeling to the strength of fact. Our trust is not in *our hold*, but in the strong Hand which will never let us go. "Fear not, for I have redeemed thee!" "The Father himself loveth you!" There is a remedy both for weakness and loneliness there.'

Another silence, for which, being true friends, we did not apologise. My mind slipped back to the old days at Heatherstone, every recollection of which was now beyond expression precious. Something of this sort I said to Mary.

'I do not wonder at your feeling so,' she replied; and yet, after all, Elsie, I am not sure that those years, from eighteen to twenty, are always, or altogether the brightest, however they may seem so when we look back to them from under darker skies. One is always striving to settle questions which cannot be settled, and one's mind is full of ideals, to which outward life can by no means be brought to correspond. It's a time of waking up from

K

day dreams too, and that is never a pleasant process, though it may be a wholesome one.'

'No; for before getting thoroughly roused, one has to receive some blows from the material furniture of the world, which are decidedly more healthful than agreeable.'

Mary laughed. 'Don't you think, Elsie, that the discipline of circumstances is very often a discipline of contraries? I mean, that one gets precisely the training that one does *not* like—precisely that which touches the part of our nature which most needs bringing into order. It is such a blessing that God's hand trains us, not our own; we know so little what we need, or what we could bear! But I must go,' she added, hastily rising. 'We generally have sacred music about this time on a Sunday evening. But you look tired, darling; you had better rest a while longer.'

So I lay and listened to the sweet sounds which floated up from the open windows below, and thought of words still sweeter, which Mary had quoted—'The Father himself loveth you!' and resting in these, I was lonely no more.

.   .   .   .   .   .

The next day Dr Wilton drove me over to Ivyburn for my promised visit to Miss Melville. The memory of it has been a rest ever since, though it lasted only a week, and the days passed all too quickly. But there are some persons who seem to soothe us, whether present or absent. Everything about them is so entirely in tune, that the very thought of them harmonises the discords of our life.

Mary and I were sitting in the drawing-room the morning after my return, where, while Mrs Wilton was in some way engaged, we had been receiving a succession of callers. I think we were both a little tired, for there are few things more exhausting than entertaining un-entertainable people, and it appeared to me that most of our visitors came under that description. They seemed to have nothing to say, or, if they had, they did not take the trouble to say it; so that the benefit of their society was a subject of very doubtful speculation. Two or three there were, indeed, who talked so fast, that I had held my breath to listen; but still, quantity did not entirely atone for quality.

Altogether I am afraid the morning had left me in a very uncharitable mood, for I was just saying to Mary that such an experience always reminded me of a verse in the Psalms; 'And when he cometh to see me he speaketh vanity.'

'Are you not a little severe, Miss Ellis?' said a deep voice behind me; and, looking up, I saw Mr Grey leaning in through the half-open window.

'Why, Edward, are you there?' said Mary. 'I thought you had gone to Collington Pike.'

'No good in going to Collington or any other Pike on a sultry day like this. There's nothing to be seen but a glimmering purple haze, which I can watch as well from the garden.'

'So, having nothing better to do, you turned eavesdropper, by way of proving once more the connection between mischief and idleness?'

'Precisely. But did you never hear of an idle tongue, as well as idle hands?'

'Yes, indeed. Mary and I have just been listening to nearly a dozen. It wasn't hearing *of*, but *hearing.*

A grave look, in which a curious sparkle of the eyes expressed as much amusement as rebuke, was the only answer vouchsafed to this impertinence.

'But really, Edward,' pleaded Mary, 'you don't know in the least how wearying it is to one's spirit, and temper, and patience, to entertain a succession of morning visitors.'

'Yes, I think I do. One needs a very fresh, loving spirit, and an abundance of sympathy, to penetrate the smooth, conventional surface of things, and touch the human life that is always underneath.'

This speech was rather beyond me. It touched a point I had by no means reached. I went on with my list of grievances.

'Mary and I are both unamiable to-day—at least I am; Mary, I believe, is never anything of the kind—in the prospect of spending this evening at Arnedale, with Mrs White. If I could only divide myself for once, I should know very well what to do with my body, and what with my soul!'

'Elsie,' said Mary, shaking her head at me, 'when will you leave off making these wild speeches?'

'Not in hot weather, Mary. I can't help it. It always makes me wicked. Besides, Mrs White is just one of the people I *cannot* get on with, she is so stiff and unapproachable. She frightens me—sends me into myself.'

'Ah! you don't know Mrs White. She is very loving when you get at her; and her stiff manner proceeds, I believe, entirely from shyness.'

'Shyness!' I exclaimed in surprise.

'It's a curious fact, isn't it,' said Mr Grey, taking off his straw hat, and laying it on the window sill, 'that causes totally different will produce the same apparent results; or, rather, that opposite principles sometimes develope and find their outward expression in nearly the same form?'

'Well—for instance?'

'For instance, you meet a person who seems to you cold, and proud, and unapproachable. You shudder, as if your spiritual antennæ had touched a piece of ice. "How can people be so disagreeable?" Well, perhaps you are right; for one can't deny that there *are* disagreeable people in the world, though I suppose they all have some "angel touch," if we could only see it. Still, its just as likely that you are wrong.'

'But I don't understand ——.'

'Extreme shyness may take refuge, as it often does, in this half-defiant manner, seeking for a screen by entrenching itself behind a barrier of exaggerated self-defence. Coldness, again, is not always indifference; it may be intense timidity. Some people absolutely haven't the courage to let the love and sympathy that are in them come forth.'

'Which fact may be the origin of many false and hasty judgments,' said Mary.

'Undoubtedly.' Mr Grey made no application of his 'fact,' but my conscience did. It was a lesson upon charity which I did not soon forget.

The speaker took up his hat again, and strolled leisurely away.

'Mary,' I said, speaking on a sudden impulse, 'I wonder you and Mr Grey have never married.'

'Do you?' she replied, meeting my glance with a look as frank and simple as a child's. 'Many people have wondered at that. *I* never did.'

'What keeps him here so long then? and what has become of those systematic explorations of the neighbourhood of which he gave us such careful notice?'

'The weather has been too hot for long walks,' said Mary, answering my second question only, and smiling, I thought, rather curiously. But just then the bell rang for luncheon.

I could not quite make out the relation in which

these two stood to each other. As for Mary, she was so perfectly at her ease with Mr Grey, so entirely free from the faintest shadow of constraint, that I could not believe she either cared for him then, or ever had done so. And whether he cared for her, I could not tell. He was just one of those men about whom you never can find out anything unless they choose to let you.

'Who will drive with me this afternoon?' asked Dr Wilton, as we rose from luncheon.

'You, Elsie,' said Mrs Wilton. 'Its your duty to inhale as much north country air as you can.'

I was beginning an excuse about the heat and a headache, for these solemn drives with the Doctor were not much to my fancy; but he stopped me by saying that the carriage would be at the door at two o'clock, and he should expect me to be ready. From childhood I had never dreamed of disobeying him any more than my father.

'You shall have plenty of shade, Elsie. I'll take you round by Driver's Lane and the Woodlands. Go and get your bonnet, my child; you look as if you wanted freshening.'

'I wonder, Mary,' I said, as she wandered into my room while I prepared for my drive, 'when people will leave off keeping me in order. It seems to me as if every one thought himself or herself privileged to lecture me. Ernest does it at home, and now this Mr Grey is beginning.'

'Nay, Edward didn't mean to lecture; but—'

'Well, I never heard him speak so many consecutive words before, Mary. I hope he isn't exhausted by the effort he made for my benefit. He seems to take everything in; but he doesn't let much come out. He looks to me as if he put up his face for a screen, and sat behind it.'

'He's very good, Elsie.'

'Ah! well, I daresay; but that doesn't prevent him from being very dry. Hark! there's the phaeton. And, dear me! there's Mr Grey going too,—going to look at the purple haze from another point of view.'

'Possibly. I see papa is dismissing Thompson; so I suppose Edward is promoted to the honour of taking his place.'

But, in the course of our drive, I found that Mr Grey was not so 'dry' as I thought. Leaning forward from the back seat of the phaeton, he began a conversation with Dr Wilton which soon enlisted my eager attention. I do not remember the subject, but I can still recall the keen delight of following the argument on either side, and gleaning many new ideas for memory and thought to work upon.

How pleasant it is to listen quietly to a well-sustained conversation! I remember, even at seven or eight years old, the mortification of being prevented from doing so, by a well-meant attempt to amuse the 'poor child, who must be very tired and sleepy.' Of course there was much which the child could not understand, but it was pleasant to watch for the little bits here and there which came within comprehension ; pleasanter still, perhaps, to speculate wonderingly upon the strange, dim world which lay beyond it. How provoking—I use the word advisedly, for I am sure all the 'combativeness' of my nature was roused—to be disturbed from dreams so sweet, and asked to look at a picture-book! And now, in elder years, the same delight retains its freshness. We women are sometimes accused of being bad listeners —a slander which might be elaborately refuted, only just now I must not stop longer in my story.

The conversation was interrupted by our arrival at Woodlands, where Dr Wilton stopped to pay a professional visit.

'By the way,' he said, as he prepared to alight, 'do you know, Edward, that young Harford is down—your old school-fellow? You might as well call upon him.'

'So I might, but it's too bad to leave you alone, Miss Ellis.'

'Oh, she'll be safe enough,' said Dr Wilton. 'Frolic is a "sober, honest beast," in spite of his name, and we shall be back in five minutes. See, I'll draw you up under the shade of this old elm, Elsie, and we'll leave you to your meditations.'

Which were of home and Ernest. I leaned back in the phaeton, holding the reins listlessly in one hand, and soothed by the dreamy, drowsy sounds around. A little brook was 'singing its quiet tune' on the other side of the road—the only thing awake and active, as it seemed; for, in the sultry stillness, the very leaves were asleep, and even the grasshoppers quiet. Only in the thick boughs above me I could hear—

'That old, mysterious murmur like far seas,
  Haunting the summer noon's tranquillity.'

There are times in one's life, though they come but now and then when the 'to be' seems for a short space separated from the 'to do' and 'to suffer,'—when the rush of life is for one moment still, and we can stop to take breath, and feel the blessing of simple existence in this fair world which God has given. Such seasons we can all remember; and the thought of them, laid up among things that can never grow old, comes back to bless us still.

But my dreams, and dreams they were, rather than thoughts, were doomed to be rudely broken. Whether Frolic had been dreaming too, and had seen a terrible vision in his sleep, or whether some object of alarm, which was invisible to my eyes, had presented itself to his, I cannot say; but certain it is that, without any apparent cause, he first pricked up his ears, then laid them flat back, tossed up his head, took the bit determinedly between his teeth, and started off at a gallop.

I grasped the reins as firmly as I could; but my force was nothing against that of the powerful creature whom fear had suddenly roused to a perception of his strength. On, on, we flew—gates and hedges whirling past with dizzy speed, while I could feel nothing but the hot air rushing against my face, and the straining of the animal's head, which almost tore the reins from my fast-relaxing hold. If I could keep them from getting entangled among his feet, it would be as much as I could hope to accomplish. As to checking or guiding him, that was out of the question.

It was a moment of intense and terrible consciousness. One swift glance upward—one desperate grasp of a strong stay—there was time for that, but no more. And yet the minutes between Frolic's first start and his final pulling up seemed to me like long ages,—a dark, endless dream of horror and death. There could not have been many of them, however; for his fiery speed soon abated, and he suffered himself to be seized and held by a labouring man, who ran to my help from a field by the roadside.

Trembling in every limb—for I was weak still from my recent illness—I managed to get out of the phaeton and stumble through a gate which stood open temptingly near. I remember throwing myself on the cool, fresh grass, and wondering, dreamily, whether any one would come to seek me; and then, I suppose, I must have fainted, for I was conscious of nothing more, till I heard some one at my side asking if I was hurt. I looked up to have my eyes met by those of Edward Grey.

' I don't know. I am not quite sure yet,' I replied,

forgetting, in my confusion, that I had met with nothing to hurt me. He smiled. There was kindliness in the smile, at any rate, whatever else there might be.

'Then I don't think you are much hurt: try to get up.'

I remembered afterwards the matter-of-fact abruptness of this speech, and was considerably amused thereat. At present I simply obeyed.

'Now, are there any bones broken?' he asked, mischievously, when he had helped me to rise, and still half-supported me.

'No, thank God!' I involuntarily exclaimed; but the sudden rush of feeling was too much, and I could not help a strong shudder.

'You are faint, sit down again; excuse me,' and my bonnet was untied in a moment.

'No, I'm not going to faint, I never did such a thing in my life, I said, making a desperate effort after my voice.

'Good reasoning! Keep quiet, will you? I'm afraid your memory doesn't reach back more than two minutes.' I believe I attempted to maintain, woman-like, that I had not fainted; but I was again requested to 'keep quiet.'

But now came up Dr Wilton and young Mr Harford, and, in the confusion of questions and replies and suggestions, quietness was no longer possible, and I was obliged to rouse myself and put on my bonnet, which Mr Grey had all this time been dangling irreverently by one string, much as if he was afraid to touch it.

Frolic, meanwhile, had been soothed and patted into composure, and now stood the very picture of meekness, drooping his head as if in repentance for the wild freak he had played. And we drove home without further mischance.

But it was curious how, all the evening after, my hand seemed to keep upon it the light touch of Edward Grey's, as it rested there for one second when he placed me in the phaeton. And I could not help thinking how strange it was that, twice in this same day, he had seemed to take me under his management, as no one ever did before. A thought which frequently recurred during the remainder of my visit.

XII.

ALONE AGAIN.

'I hear a sound of marriage bells.'

—TENNYSON.

CHAPTER XII.

ALONE AGAIN.

EST, however pleasant, cannot, in the present constitution of things, be very long continued. My visit to Greyslope came to an end, and, with restored health and vigour, I bade adieu once more to the blue hills and quiet valleys of my native county, and returned to the old writing-desk, with its piles of parchment, which seemed for a time more uninteresting than ever.

It was very wrong and thankless—so I reasoned with myself many times in the day—but I could not help feeling as if the common world had somehow gone further off, and my friends, I could not tell why, were grown 'a little colder, and the least less dear.' Looking back now, I can see that the change was in myself. We often think the sunlight has faded, when it is only our own eyes that have grown dim.

L

However, happily perhaps for me, I had little time
for day-dreams. A sterner reality soon absorbed my
thoughts and care ; and dark days followed, which were
none the *less* dark because of the joy in which they
ended. 'The night of weeping' is always dreary while it
lasts, though we may look hopefully forward to the 'joy
which cometh in the morning.'

My brother, my darling brother, the shield and sunshine of my lonely life, became suddenly and seriously
ill. Typhoid fever, in its most virulent form, brought him
to the brink of the grave, and all hope of his recovery
hung upon so slender a thread, that it seemed a mere
mockery to indulge it. And, as he would have no nurse
but myself and our good landlady, my own strength
was soon nearly exhausted by anxiety and watching.

How sad it was to see the manly form laid prostrate
—the blue eyes vacant and wandering ! How painful
to listen to the wild raving of delirium—to hear the
moaning, pitiful cry for 'Grace, Gracie darling,' which
told how that one name was hidden away in the heart's
secret depths ! But when the danger was over, and the
long hours of convalescence followed, how great was my
thankfulness to see that not only was bodily strength
returning, but that spiritual health also was vouchsafed
by the Spirit of power and life !

The little Bible, our mother's dying gift to her boy,
was searched now with diligence and prayer ; and from
his silent sickroom my brother came forth another man,

changed by His mighty working, who 'maketh all things new.' And when, as soon as possible after his recovery, we knelt together at that holy table where I had so often prayed alone, my full heart could find no other utterance than in the words of one of the Psalms for the day: 'It is a good thing to give thanks unto the Lord; yea, a joyful and pleasant thing it is to be thankful.'

Ernest's strength was slow in returning, and, by his doctor's order, we spent some weeks in the autumn at a small watering-place on the Welsh coast. One day, as I gathered up his letters for the post, my glance fell upon the direction, 'Miss Munroe, Howard Place, Everton, Liverpool.'

Our eyes met, but we did not speak. Only, as his hand was laid upon mine, I could feel that it trembled.

We both watched anxiously for the approach of the letter-carrier by the earliest post which could possibly bring a reply. He passed our lodging without stopping, however, and on the second morning brought only the blue business-looking packages, with their stiff upright superscription, which even Ernest for once admitted to be uninteresting. On the third day we were together upon the shore, when we saw him approach our door,—for Liverpool letters were delivered in the afternoon, and this was our usual time for exercise. Ernest sprang up the rocky path which led from the sands to the village, with more vigour than he had shown since his illness.

He soon returned, giving me a letter for myself, and then walked to a little distance to read his own.

Mine, from our hostess at Wavertree, was soon despatched, and, seating myself on a fragment of rock, I looked out upon the beauty of sea and sky, and strove to quiet a little trembling of heart, by resting on the strength of Him who made them. Surely it was His glory which fell upon water and shore, as they lay so fair and still in the soft golden haze of October; and surely His light was around me in more senses than one; for I felt that, even as the sunshine touched the grey rocks into beauty, so whatever might be hard or sharp in the future, would be brightened by His presence.

At length, when my patience was pretty nearly exhausted, I saw Ernest coming towards me. Had he heard from Grace? No need to ask, for there was a glow on his face, to which the sunshine could have added nothing.

'God has given me a great blessing, Elsie,' he said, as he stooped to kiss my forehead, 'the greatest He *could* have given after the gift of His own love in Christ.'

'I know,' I answered, looking up to him with a smile, which shone, I fear, through tears; 'the barrier is removed; you are made one at last; I am to welcome Grace as my sister.'

Poor Grace! It makes my heart ache even now to think of all she must have gone through at this time. For it is no light thing to follow the right, when it has in other eyes the semblance of wrong, and to bear with unanswering patience the bitterness of harsh judgment and misconstruction. The lesson of the 37th Psalm is not learned without tears and pain : 'Rest in the Lord, and wait patiently for him : he shall bring forth thy righteousness as the light, and thy judgment as the noonday.' Probably there comes a time, in the history of each one of us, when we stand face to face with duty, which it seems that we alone can recognise—called to be true to ourselves, even at the risk of seeming false to what is dearer than ourselves.

It is easy to say that, in such a case, duty is plain and will bring its own reward ; but the balance of conflicting claims is not thus easily settled. There comes, first, much failing of heart and of hope, much walking in darkness with weary feet, many an hour when sense and strength seem alike to fail, and we can only cry in our helplessness, ' O Lord, I am oppressed, undertake for me !' And when at length the prayer is answered, and the 'way wherein we should walk' is made plain before us, even then the battle is not won, for the struggle between feeling and principle ends not in a day. God's grace, indeed, may give us the victory ; but the joy of it is not yet.

So I know these autumn months must have passed very sadly for poor Grace. Yet, after all, 'what do they know who have not suffered ?' Already she had learned the new song which those sing who have 'passed from death unto life ;' but now God would lead her on to the deeper harmonies which are brought out only by sorrow.

Already she had put on the heavenly armour; but He, the Captain of her salvation, himself made perfect through suffering, knew that it must be tempered and brightened by conflict. And when I saw how her character had gained in strength and dignity, as well as in beauty, how its hardness was softened and its immaturity mellowed, I recognised the touch of His hand, who was preparing the chosen instrument for the life-work which He would appoint.

Yes, it was well for her that she had suffered, and well for many sad hearts which should hereafter be cheered by her gentle ministry.

But now, for the present, at least, the clouds had rolled away from her sky, and left the sunny blue brighter in contrast. Winter was gladdened by a joy of its own, to which spring, in due time, brought deeper fulness, and sealed with holier blessing. For, when 'primrose stars' were gleaming through the hedgerows, and cowslips nodding in the meadows, there came a sound of merry bells from the old Church upon the hill, and Mr Kenway's deep voice pronounced the marriage blessing over the two now made for ever one.

Kenneth, Janet, and I, were very busy, during the brief absence of the newly-married couple, in preparing the home which the two former were to share, for Grace could not be separated from her brother, nor Janet from

Kenneth. And I too might have had, as I well knew, a welcome corner by the ingle nook ; but I felt that it was best and wisest for me to continue in the lodging which I had hitherto occupied.

And now began my life of solitary spinsterhood. Not very solitary, however, for Ernest passed my door twice a day on his way to and from town, and if he had not time to stop, he sent up to my window a smile which was like a glint of sunshine. And I was often at Claremont Terrace, where Grace's welcome was always as warm and sisterly as heart could wish.

But still, to all intents and purposes, I lived alone. Which of us, after all, in the deepest sense, does not ? And, perhaps, in my quiet room, I was less really lonely than many who dwell among alien hearts, and respond listlessly to greetings wherein is no kindness.

Yet there are many temptations and evils in a solitary life. It is not only that you choose the warmest corner and the most comfortable chair, by undisputed right! but you can indulge the mood of the moment, whatever that may be, without thought of another's pleasure, or fear of another's pain. There is no necessity to restrain the expression of impatience or irritability. You are never contradicted. You nurse your pet theories, till they take possession of your whole being, and no one shows you how difficult, or even impossible, it may be to reduce them to practice. You look at a subject on one side only, because there is no one at hand, with sympathies and antipathies the exact opposite of your own, to turn it round and inside out, and show you the other. You are never interrupted. No one wakes you out of a delicious day-dream, or breaks the thread of a philosophical speculation, by asking whether you want fish for dinner, or whether the bonnet you wore on Sunday is not growing a little shabby. No one tries your patience by an April temper, from which you never know whether to expect showers or sunshine at any given moment.

And, although these things are nowise pleasant in themselves, they yet do effectual service in the refining of character. The hourly thorn may be as much God's instrument as the daily cross. If the infirmities and peculiarities of those we live with supply, in some senses, the best correction for our own, there is reason to fear lest we should live alone till we are unfit to live with others.

But the theory of compensation holds good here, as elsewhere; and if solitude has its dangers, it certainly has its pleasures, and may have its blessings. At any rate, we know in whose hand is the ordering of our outward lot, and that the words are as true for each of us as they were for the Church of Sardis, ' I know where thou dwellest.' And, with the remembrance of this perfect knowledge, we can never be alone.

XIII.

WOMEN AND WORK.

'The honest, earnest man must stand and work ;
  The woman also: otherwise she drops
 At once below the dignity of man,
  Accepting serfdom.'

—E. B. BROWNING.

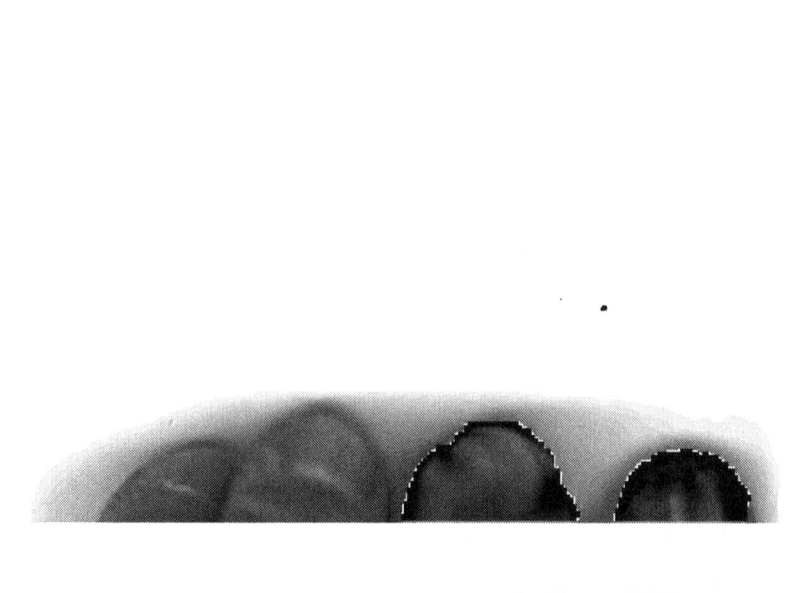

CHAPTER XIII.

WOMEN AND WORK.

 WAS not, in point of fact, long left alone, even in outward seeming. What do you say to a little society for a change?' asked Mrs Claude, one day, when her pretty grey ponies were drawn up at my door, and her two youngest children were disturbing the repose of my grave cat, who, not being accustomed to any very violent demonstrations of friendship, testified her disapprobation of the same, by deliberately walking away from them.

'Our neighbours, the Hamiltons, are in great distress just now. You know the girls, don't you? You have met them at our house. (Bertie, my dear, don't pull pussie's tail; she doesn't like it.) Well, Mr Hamilton died suddenly about a month ago, leaving his affairs in most inextricable confusion. It is thought there will be nothing left for Helen and Kate, except a few hundreds which were settled on their mother at her marriage ; enough to keep the wolf from the door, certainly, but nothing to live upon. They must do something for themselves ; but what ? (Take care, Willie darling ; you'll upset Miss Ellis's work-basket.)'

A catastrophe I had been fearing for some time. But mothers are never disturbed by such little interludes, and Mrs Claude went on with her story.

'Poor girls ! they are left very desolate : not orphans only, but, it seems, almost without friends. They have only one uncle ; in India, if he is anywhere ; but he hasn't been heard of for many years ; so that, except my husband, who was Mr Hamilton's most intimate friend, there is really no one for them to look up to.'

'Are they quite young ?' I asked.

'Helen is two-and-twenty, and Kate just seventeen —hardly out of the schoolroom. They are staying with us at present ; but our house will be full when the boys come home at Christmas, and we thought it would be nice if they might share your lodging for a time, till they can arrange their plans, and see a little before them. You don't object ?'

'Certainly not. I shall be very glad of a break in my solitude.'

'Ah ! I thought so. Then it will be a pleasant arrangement for both parties. And oh ! Elsie,' she added, 'perhaps you will be able to tell them, better than I, where to look for true comfort in their grief. Helen, I think, knows; but I am not quite so sure of Kate, and she may listen more readily to you who have, in some measure, drunk of the same cup.'

And so the long-tailed greys trotted away, and my poor old cat was left in peace.

But I could not resume my writing without first asking strength and guidance, higher than my own, for the new life which seemed opening before me. Oh! how sweet it is, whenever we come to any bit of work that is too hard for us, just to go and ask 'our Father' to help us in it! The little child feels that he has no strength or wisdom of his own; but he knows where to look for both. 'Show me how to do this; it is too difficult for me.' And the Father bends down in pitying love and patience, and the child stands meekly by, helpless and yet trustful, while the burden is lifted by a stronger hand, and the tangled threads fall into their proper place.

Helen Hamilton had always strongly attracted me, whenever I met her, as I often did, at the house of our friend, Mrs Claude. She did not possess either the brilliancy or the beauty of her younger sister, for Kate was one of the gifted few who are peeresses of society in their own right. But Helen reminded me of a white rose, pure and pale; not asserting itself, even by its sweetness; not startling, even by its beauty; but blooming softly in the shade, filling the quiet place with light.

The shadow of Helen's earliest recollection seemed to have rested upon her whole life. It was that of a darkened room, whose stillness was broken only by sobs, where lay a motionless figure, pale as marble, and almost as cold. And the little Helen was lifted up to press one last kiss upon those white lips, and to receive one look of love from those fast-glazing eyes. And then the baby Kate was brought, and the same look, only more tender now, more full of unutterable yearning, rested on her also. And after this the children saw their mother no more.

So Helen grew up, grave and staid, her father's companion, and her little sister's guardian. Older and sadder than her years, she seemed to have been hardly ever a child. She made few friends, though her acquaintances might be numbered by scores, and of these, each one innocently thought he knew all about her, that there was to be known. It was a delusion which Helen never took any pains to dispel. She went on her own way, and but few suspected that it was not theirs.

Society, in the meantime, was well pleased with the graceful Miss Hamilton. A little quiet, perhaps; now and then a little cold; but these are trifles. It is not the fashion now-a-days to betray much feeling. She was amiable and intelligent; could converse agreeably enough; could play and sing well; and society did not require from her much more. Young ladies envied the quiet self-possession with which their own rapid, ill-assured manner contrasted so unfavourably. Young gentlemen admired her fine figure, and her father's reputed wealth.

Papas called her 'a sensible girl, with no enthusiastic nonsense about her;' and even mammas patronized her a good deal, especially if they had no daughters of their own. Some few there were who watched her with painful, prayerful interest, and questioned anxiously what might be the discipline, or what the work, in store for her in the future.

The one, indeed, had declared itself plainly enough, but the other was difficult to determine; and once more, a week or two after the Hamiltons were settled at Wavertree, the question of possibilities and capabilities was discussed in my little sitting-room. I felt scarcely less interested in it, than on a former memorable day when it touched upon my personal need.

As for Kate,—look at her, sitting there in the firelight glow, which seems to fall with a half-caressing touch upon her perfect face and figure, set off by their dark draping. It is hard to connect that fairy form with any idea of work. She seems a creature made to be petted and cared for,—every stone in life's rough pathway moved from before those tender little feet. So at least thinks Helen, who, in the intense devotion of her nature, was preparing herself to work, and toil, and watch, till strength and youth were spent, rather than let her cherished darling take the smallest share of the burden.

Besides, 'Kate is such a child,' thought the grave older sister, in the antiquity of her twenty-three summers; for it is difficult to believe, that those whom we remember in the short petticoat stage of existence, can ever grow out of it. On this subject, however, 'the child' herself, as is frequently the case, entertained different notions. She looked up now, her face a little flushed and eager, her large grey eyes glowing with a rather unquiet light.

'What do you mean me to do, Helen?' she asked.

'I don't think you need do anything, darling. I hope I shall be able to earn enough for us both.'

'But I don't like that; I won't have it,' said the wilful child. 'It's very good of you, Helen; but I would rather work for myself.'

How well I understood her feeling! It had been my own in days not long gone by. But Helen looked a little disappointed; perhaps there was a touch of pride in her self-denial. She liked to think that her sister was dependent on her unaided exertions. And it is so pleasant to be necessary to those we love!

'What would you like to do, Kate?' I asked.

'It's hardly a question of liking, Miss Ellis. I want work of some kind, it doesn't much matter what, if I can only do it.'

Ay, if!—an important condition. But there were hundreds of women, in Liverpool alone, ready to reiterate the same painful cry, 'We want work.' And, 'We want workers,' was the answering echo, from workhouse and hospital, from counting-house and shop; 'but then they must be trained. No mere beginners will do for us. We want skilled hands, and practised heads.'

And here was the difficulty. Helen and Kate were both well educated, in the ordinary acceptation of this much-abused term,—that is to say, they had spent as much time, in learning to do many things tolerably, as, if devoted to any one particular branch of study, would probably have enabled them to excel in it. But they knew nothing so thoroughly, as to be able to fall back upon it now, when their need was the sorest.

'How would you like to learn law-copying with me, Kate?'

Poor Kate looked rather blank. 'And all my accomplishments must go for nothing!'

'Nay, dear, they need not, if you are so sure of any one of them as to be able to teach it.'

She shook her head sadly. 'I see now how miserably superficial they all are.'

'Besides, don't you think you are rather young for a governess? Suppose you work with me in the meantime, until—'

'Until I grow old and grey, and experienced-looking? Very well, perhaps it would be best.'

So the matter was settled—for Kate, but not for Helen. I had felt the disadvantage of beginning my work when too old for it, and could not advise her to make a similar attempt.* She herself inclined to teaching, being, as she said, fond of children. So we inserted

---

* Sixteen is the best age to begin to learn law-copying. A law stationer would not receive a pupil who was over twenty.

M

and answered advertisements in the various local papers, and made application and inquiry, till we were all three sick at heart, but, alas! without success. Almost every mother required some accomplishment which Helen did not thoroughly possess; and as she was too honest to profess what she could not make good, every hopeful negotiation was broken off when it reached a certain point; while, again, for the instruction of very little children, who needed no accomplishments, the renumeration offered was so scanty, as to be a mere mockery in exchange for strength and time.

'I must give up this plan,' said poor Helen, at length; 'it is evidently fruitless. I must bring my ideas down to my circumstances, and begin two or three rounds lower in the social ladder. No disgrace, after all; for the work we can do is always noble, and, as for the pleasantness, I must put that out of my calculations.'

True woman! true heroine! taking up the thorny cross with a smile, and wearing it as if it were a crown.

And she acted upon her words nobly, if not wisely. Through the kindness of Mr Claude, she obtained introductions to several gentlemen, who were in the habit of offering employment to women, to whom she determined to offer her services, either as book-keeper or corresponding clerk. I ventured to inquire if she had studied book-keeping; but, in her utter ignorance of business matters, she did not seem to comprehend that any special study could be necessary, as she 'had always been fond of figures.' And I thought it might perhaps be best to let her make the trial.

So we set forth one morning, Helen and I, from our unfashionable suburb, on an expedition to town, from which she, in her secret heart, shrunk, I knew, more than words could tell, though few would have guessed as much from her calm face and self-possessed bearing.

Our first call was on a Mr Hayward, the head of a large 'ladies outfitting establishment,' whose advertisement for an accountant, and the salary offered, had excited Helen's hopes. Yes, Mr Hayward was at home; and we were forthwith ushered through endless staircases and lobbies to that gentleman's private office. He looked up from his desk as we entered,—a thin, spare-built man, with a face full of wrinkles, every one expressive of busy energy and shrewdness, and a 'shock' of dust-coloured hair, which looked as if it had no time to be flat, but must needs be restless, like its owner.

'Be seated, ladies,' said a sharp, wiry voice, quite in keeping with figure and face; and, after nodding towards two chairs, the head turned to its desk again, and seemed absorbed in a ledger. We waited till I, at least, began to feel impatient, even to the very tips of my fingers; but still the occupant of the desk appeared unconscious of our presence. At length he laid down his pen, pushed up his spectacles, and inquired, drily, 'if we wanted anything.'

I explained that my young friend had seen Mr

Hayward's advertisement for a book-keeper, and hoped she might be allowed to take the vacant place.

'Ah! Been in any situation before?'

'No,' said Helen, in a voice which, to any but dense ears, would have spoken volumes.

The sharp eyes glanced at her crape. 'Of course you understand book-keeping?'

'Yes,' said Helen, looking very doubtfully at the ledger, which seemed very different from her housekeeping book.

'Book-keeping by double entry?' pursued her interrogator, while the grey eyes never wavered in their scrutiny.

'No; I—that is, I have not.'

'Ah! I see,' said Mr Hayward, rising and touching a bell; 'same tale over again—same tale! You're the fourth applicant this morning, and not one seems even to know the requirements of the place. It's a queer thing—very—that women should be so ignorant.' (Not so very queer after all, my good sir! Are you teaching your own daughters, if you have any, to be much wiser?) 'Show these ladies out. Good morning, ma'am; good morning.'

Poor Helen drew her crape veil over her face, and traversed staircases and lobbies in silence. I took her arm in mine, and spoke as cheeringly as I could.

'Never mind one failure, dear; remember Bruce and the spider. You have a knowledge of French and

German ; let us seek out this gentleman who wants a corresponding clerk ; you have a note to him from Mr Claude.'

We turned to a large drapery establishment, which gave employment to between fifty and sixty young women, and where Mr Claude thought the firm might not object to have their correspondence conducted by a lady, if she proved herself equal to their requirements.

'Half an hour too late,' was the laconic reply to our application. 'Very sorry, ma'am, if you're disappointed; good morning.' And a personage, with a profusion of rings and chains, bowed us off the premises.

'Never mind ; there are more names on the list. Let me see it. Ah! this seems likely : Neal and Co. ; just three numbers further up, and the same kind of thing. Haven't you a note to Mr Neal ? Keep up your heart, dear, for one more trial.'

There was something encouraging in the aspect of the office into which we were ushered upon this occasion. It was not nearly so gloomy and dark as the others had been, and there were unmistakeable traces that its occupant was a man of refinement and some literary taste. The empty room was visibly impressed with the personality of its absent master. We drew our own conclusions, and grew hopeful.

'Mr Neal ?' I said, when, after we had waited a few minutes, a gentleman entered, and looked from one to the other, with a face of polite inquiry.

'My name is Hope.   Mr Neal is not in at present ;
but perhaps I may be able to give you the information
you require.'

He was a tall, finely-formed man, with a face to
which one instinctively gave confidence, almost without
knowing why.   I explained the object of our visit, and
gave Mr Claude's note of introduction.   Mr Hope looked
up from it with a smile.

'Perhaps you would be kind enough,' he said to
Helen, 'to write me a copy of this note.'

He placed a chair for her at the desk ; and then,
turning to me, chatted pleasantly until she had finished
her copy.   She wrote it quickly and well, in a clear
plain hand, which might be read at a glance, though her
utmost efforts at self-control could not prevent some of
the letters from being a little tremulous.

'That is very good,' said her examiner, looking it
over with a satisfied smile.   'A young lady came for
trial yesterday, whose hand was a series of impossible
angles.   Now turn it into French, please.'

Poor Helen felt her cheeks grow hot ; but she took
up her pen, and resumed her task.

'If I had only kept up my French better!' she
thought ; but she had never cared for it in comparison
with German, and after a residence of some months
abroad, had never taken the trouble to speak it.   Too
late now to remedy the deficiency !   However, she
finished her translation, though with a miserable con-

sciousness that it was inaccurate, if not ungrammatical.
Mr Hope examined it more careful than we thought was
at all needful. I felt sure afterwards that he had been
studying how to express his verdict in a form as little
unpleasant as might be.

'I could do it so much better in German,' pleaded
Helen, when at length he looked up and met her wistful
glance.

'Ah! I don't wonder. The grand old Deutsch, with
its rugged strength and kindliness, is so much more
attractive. But, you see, French is more useful for
commercial purposes; and I'm afraid—' He looked at
the letter, and hesitated.

'I should not be able to undertake what you require,'
said Helen, taking refuge from her confusion in a touch
of stateliness. But Mr Hope, I felt sure, was too keen
an observer not to notice the convulsive movement of
the features, even through the friendly veil, which she
hastily drew down.

'I hope,' he answered kindly, 'that you will soon
meet with some more suitable employment.'

How much the pain of that refusal was softened by
gentle words! Pity their sweet music is not oftener
heard in this harsh world! But Helen's reply was a
silent inclination of her head, and a retreat as speedy as
could be accomplished.

Once more in the street, with its noise and turmoil.
Poor Helen grew sick at heart, as the hurrying tide of

human life swept past her, and seemed, to her morbid imagination, to leave her stranded on a dreary shore. She said nothing ; but there was language more forcible than words in the disconsolate droop of the tall figure, which was wont to hold itself so erect.

'I think, dear, we won't attempt anything more to-day.'

'No, indeed,' she answered, with a ghastly effort at a smile ; but her voice would not serve her further.

'Would you mind waiting here for a few minutes?' I led the way into a bookseller's shop, where I made a trifling purchase. 'I have a little business in Lord Street, but I shall return soon.'

I saw that her strength was almost spent, and I wished for her the relief of solitude,—such solitude, at least, as can be secured in the mindst of a crowd. She was looking very pale when I returned to her ; but there was a light in her eyes which must have been the reflection of some inner brightness, since there was nothing in her outward world at that moment to call it forth. But God's own children can never be entirely desolate. Sorrow and loneliness there may be for them as for others ; for the words which have floated down to us over the waste of centuries, find their echo still, and it is as true now, as in the days of old, that we must, 'through much tribulation,' enter into the kindgom. But in all this is the 'life of the spirit ;' and even in darkest moments, we know that the Lord is 'very pitiful, and of tender mercy,' and will not suffer us to be tempted 'above that we are able to bear.'

'Can you go home now, dear? There's an omnibus just ready to start from Castle Street. If we walk quickly, we shall be in time for it.'

'Oh, I would rather walk out than drive, Elsie; I'm not at all tired.'

'Then you ought to be. No; I won't sanction such an unnecessary expenditure of strength. It's a good deal more precious than pence. Come.' And as we walked out of the shop, I whispered, 'Keep a brave heart, Helen; it's "always darkest before the dawning."'

But I did not think my words were to be so speedily verified. Kate met us, on our return, with a face as bright as a May morning, and a rather incoherently expressed hope that we had not been successful.

'No, indeed,' said her sister; 'but, Kate—'

She was interrupted by a shower of kisses, and an assurance that she was a 'dear stupid old thing!' At the same moment I heard Grace's silvery tones in the sitting-room, and gained from her the key to Kate's extravagances. A neighbour had asked her to recommend a daily governess for her two little girls; and as the lady valued Christian principle more than accomplishments, and was willing to employ masters to supplement Helen's deficiencies, Grace thought there was every reason to hope that she would be engaged. The salary offered was perfectly satisfactory.

Helen listened to all this with bent head and drooping eyes, saying not a word. She flashed a look at Grace, when the latter had ceased speaking, but the quivering lips uttered no sound. And then she rushed off to her room, and we saw her no more till dinner.

But in the evening, as we sat alone together (for Kate had returned with Grace to spend the day at Claremont Terrace), she opened her little Bible at the tenth verse of the 27th Psalm: 'When my father and my mother forsake me, the Lord taketh me up.'

'He has been true to His word to-day, Elsie. How lovingly, how tenderly His faithfulness rebukes our unbelief! That verse is the orphan's heritage, is it not?' she added, bending over it with glowing eyes,—'The Lord taketh me up.'

Yes; and there is fulness in the words beyond any portion of this world's giving. The mother bends to the wistful little face that looks up to her through tears, and raises to her arms the wearied, frightened child who pleads to be 'taken up;' and in that close embrace there is shelter, and safety, and rest.

Even so, but far more tenderly, does our Father 'take up' the desolate ones, who know no other refuge, folding around them His everlasting arms, supplying all their need, and soothing all their fear.

XIV.

NEW YEAR'S EVE.

'The stricken heart, bereft
Of all its brood of singing hopes, and left
'Mid leafless boughs, a cold, forsaken nest.
With snow-flakes in it—folded in thy breast,
Doth lose its deadly chill: and grief that creeps
  Unto thy side for shelter, finding there
The wound's deep cleft, forgets its moan, and weeps
  Calm, quiet tears: and on thy forehead care
  Hath looked, until its thorns, no longer bare,
Put forth pale roses.'

       —Poems by the Author of the *Patience of Hope.*

CHAPTER XIV.

NEW YEAR'S EVE.

T was New Year's Eve, not the first, but the second after Helen and Kate had been left fatherless. The year had rolled over very peacefully, bringing to us all much quiet happiness, and certainly a true affection for one another. Kate, indeed, tried both her sister and myself no little by her wild, wilful ways; but no one could help loving her, spoiled child though she was; for, with all her faults, she possessed the elements of a noble character. There was an unconscious fascination about her, which one could neither describe nor analyse,—a power which some few possess, and which may be independent alike of beauty and of talent, though in her case it was combined with both. It is a rare mingling of many gifts; but always a dangerous one to its possessor, unless God's grace chasten and consecrate it.

However, Kate kept steadily to her work; which
was more than one could have expected from a creature
so utterly undisciplined, and so little accustomed to
consider anything beyond the pleasure of the passing
moment.   But it was the only thing she did keep to,
except, indeed, her friendships, which, when once formed,
were as true as steel.

We were a pleasant little party in the drawing-room
at Claremont Terrace that last evening of the year.
There was Grace, retaining a touch of girlishness even
in her placid, matronly dignity,—her fair hair and glowing
colour set off by the blue dress she wore ; and her voice,
like a sweet, soft summer wind, the unconscious echo of
her thought.   And there, in the corner near the fire, was
Kenneth's couch, and opposite to it a low easy chair,
tenanted by one whom all. had learned to love, though
to me only she was a friend of 'lang syne'—familiar
in the dear old days that were past.   For Miss Melville
was one of our gathered group.

Business had brought her unexpectedly to Liverpool,
and Ernest had insisted that she should stay with him
over Christmas and the New Year, before returning to
the solitude of Ivyburn.   So she remained, an honoured
guest, whose presence deepened our Christmas joy.   And
indeed, as she sat there, in the grey poplin and soft white
shawl, which were my earliest ideal of what a lady's dress
should be, I could have fancied myself a very child again,
instead of a grave, sober woman, verging towards thirty

—'ten times more proper than Miss Melville,' as Kate had that morning informed me.

Kate herself looked radiant this evening, moving about with her free, stately step,—a bit of glowing geranium brightening her slight mourning dress. And yet, to my thinking, the elder sister was still the fairer, with her calm face, and calmer heart, and the low, gentle voice, which seemed ever to dwell sheltered from the 'strife of tongues' around it. There was a wavering colour in her cheeks to-night, which witnessed of excitement she could with difficulty control. And no wonder; for the last hours of the old year were to bring her, as she hoped, a joy which should gladden all the new, and many another besides.

Some few months before Mr Hamilton's death, Helen had been engaged, with his full sanction, to a young clergyman of great promise and usefulness, who was at that time curate of the Church they were in the habit of attending. But his health failed from over-exertion in preaching, and the exhausting labour of a crowded town parish; and, by medical advice, he had spent two years at Mauritius, as tutor in an English family residing there. Helen heard from him regularly, however, and his letters brought good news of returning strength and vigour. And now, on the last day of the old year, the vessel in which he was to return, was expected in port, and Ernest had gone to meet him on his arrival, and bring him up to Claremont Terrace; for his own home was in the south of England, and Grace's hospitality would not permit him to try the contingency of comfort which might be offered by an hotel.

We were all anxiously listening for the sound of wheels, which should announce the arrival of the stranger. Helen, indeed, reminded me more than once that it was very possible the packet might be delayed, even after she had been signalled at the mouth of the river; but this grave assurance did not impose either upon herself or me, for I could see her colour rise and fade, as carriage after carriage approached and passed; while the steel crochet-hook she was driving industriously through some bright-coloured silk, trembled a little now and then, and more than once struck work altogether.

'Let us have some music,' said Miss Melville, at last; and the proposal was hailed as a relief by every one. Grace sang one or two songs, and then Helen and Kate sat down to play a duet. I cannot tell how Helen accomplished her part, for I felt too restless even to listen, and discovered that the Berlin pattern I was attempting to work, had arrived at a state of most hopeless confusion. I laid it down in despair; and, glancing across the room as I did so, saw Kenneth leaning back upon his couch, looking pale, and, I thought, very weary. I crossed over to him, and asked if he were tired.

'Not physically, Elsie; but once in a while I get a little weary in mind. Don't you know that feeling?'

Did I not? But Kenneth seemed always so peaceful

and bright, that such words sounded strange from him. I sat down on a low stool 'by his side, and we talked under cover of the music. Many things had served to draw us very closely together, and Kenneth had taken me into his confidence more than once before.

' The New Years always find me here, Elsie,' he said now, turning his large eyes wistfully upon my face, while his thin fingers clasped each other, till they grew white with the tension.

'" Behold, we count them happy which endure,"' I answered, gently ; for I knew the sweet Bible words would soothe him better than any of mine.

' Ah ! yes ; but, after all, it's easier to take up the cross, and walk or work, than to lie still upon it and wait.'

' How much easier ! But if God appoints us the harder task, does He not promise the greater strength ? " As *thy* day "—don't you like that, Kenneth ?—not another's need, but our own—sharp, and pressing, and secret ; known only to God, but always to Him, and always met."'

' Ah ! yes,' he answered, taking up the thought, and following it out. ' He can tell exactly what our days are,—the dreary sunset, and the drearier dawn ; the bright, green places here and there, and the desert land "that is not sown." His eye follows us everywhere. Thank you for reminding me of that, Elsie. One need not shrink from anything that He knows. And yet— and yet, self-will dies very slowly ; and just when you think you are ready to take your "days" from God's hand, and rest in His ordering of them, you find you are not.'

And again the wearied look came back, and the pale lips quivered.

'But, dear Kenneth, will not He, our Father, end the strife for us, if we put ourselves into His hand? I often think we might have more power over besetting sin, whatever it may be—pride, or self-will, or impatience,— if we would only ask *hopefully* for it—if we would just let God's strength work in us, and through us. We pray to be made "vessels meet for his use;" and shall we not believe that He, the Potter, has power over the clay?'

'Ah! I like that so much, Elsie. "He is able to subdue all things unto himself"—even the strength of our evil nature; so we need not let that discourage us. But look—they are wanting you to sing. Now go; you have done me good.'

So I left him to rest, and joined the group at the piano.

'Sing with me, Elsie,' said Grace; 'choose which you like best from these. Don't you think they are very long?' she added, in a lower tone; 'the packet was expected early this morning, and now it's nearly nine.' And she went to give further expression to her anxiety, as we English are so apt to do, by an energetic poking of the fire. Our open grates are, in some sense, a sort of national safety-valve.

Helen had slipped from the room when our song was finished; and I knew, by her stedfast look on her return, that she had been to seek the sure refuge, which is never sought in vain. And as she passed Miss Melville's chair, I heard the latter softly whisper, 'What time I am afraid, I will trust in Thee.'

Ten o'clock came and passed. We did not attempt to talk now, but sat in silence—Helen with her hand clasped in mine. Only Kate now and then broke out into some wild sally, which called forth smiles in which there was no merriment. But she stopped suddenly in one of these, for we heard the crash of Ernest's latchkey in the door, and knew that now, at last, he had returned —and alone.

'You must have been right about the packet, Helen dear, said Grace, as she rose to open the drawing-room door; 'it has been detained very likely by a fog in the river.'

'Yes,' said Helen, dreamily. But the marble against which she leaned was not whiter than her face, and I could hear her quick breathing half across the room. Grace had closed the door after her; but still we could hear the voices in the hall—Ernest's low and hurried, hers at first in rapid questioning, and then, as I thought, slightly raised, with an exclamation of distress.

'There must be something wrong,' said Helen, speaking in tones which were so absolutely clear in their intense self-restraint, that they seemed to thrill through the room. She walked to the door and threw it open. Ernest was pulling off the second sleeve of his over-coat, but he stopped midway in the operation when he saw her.

'Has the packet not come in?' she asked, still in the same voice.

'Yes.' He added no more, but stood looking at her with such a troubled, pitying face, that I saw at once there were evil tidings in store.

'Then something has happened. Henry is—tell me, tell me the worst at once,' she added, going up to him now, and laying her little hand upon his arm, with a gesture, half commanding, half imploring. Ernest took her hand, but still he did not speak.

'Tell me,' she gasped again. 'But no—I know,' she almost shrieked, 'it is the worst, isn't it, the very worst that could have happened?' I saw Ernest bend his head, but this was all his answer.

Poor Helen; she asked no more. She did not scream, or moan, or faint; she stood as if she had been turned to stone—her white lips half parted, her eyes wild and fixed.

'It is not true,' she murmured, 'it cannot be true. Say it is not,' she added, with a ghastly smile, which made me shiver.

'My poor Helen,' said Grace, folding her arms tenderly round her, 'God has taken him to himself.'

She smiled again, a strange, wandering smile, and shook her head sadly.

'Come with me, dear,' said Miss Melville, stepping forward into the hall, and taking hold of her hand as if she had been a child. She obeyed mechanically, and suffered herself to be led upstairs, and laid upon the couch in Miss Melville's room. Grace and I followed, but it was little we could do. She lay there, still, and cold, and white, taking no notice when we spoke to her, and apparently· unconscious of all that was passing around. And we watched sadly beside her, standing as it were, with awe-struck hearts on the threshold of sorrow's shrine, and following from afar, with dumb helpless love and longing, the poor stricken one who had passed into its veiled recesses.

I stole down stairs after a time, and heard from Ernest the little he had to tell. It was a short, sad story. Mr Somers had left the Mauritius, so the captain of the vessel told him, apparently in perfect health, was seized with fever when they had been about a week at sea, and died after a few days' illness.

'He just slept away, sir, one day, after he had asked me to read him the fourteenth chapter of John out of his little Testament. And the last word I heard him say was, "Helen."'

Long, long we watched and waited during the slow hours of that dreary night. The storm rose mournfully without, and through its fitful gusts there came to us at intervals the wild sound of distant bells, ringing out their welcome to the glad New Year. I thought Helen heard them once, and shivered slightly in her death-like trance; but she never spoke, except to murmur now and then, 'that it was not true—it could not be true.' Sleep came to her at last—the sleep of mere weariness and exhaustion, just as the dawn of another morning—how like the grey future of her widowed life!—was beginning to steal through the closed blinds.

'I wonder how people live through such things; I'm sure I couldn't,' said Kate, as we rose from a late breakfast that same New Year's day. Helen was not sleeping now, but she was lying quiet, as indeed she had done from the first, and we thought it best to leave her alone. Kate had thrown herself on a stool at Miss Melville's feet, and sat gazing up into her face with a fond, wistful look, that was pretty to see; for she, too, felt the attraction of that strong, loving nature, which never failed to establish some invisible link, even with a casual acquaintance.

'My dear child,' answered the quiet voice, whose chastened tones told still of sorrow that had passed away, 'you don't know how much you could live through, in God's strength. And how good it is to remember,' she added, leaning back in her chair, and speaking rather to herself than to us, 'that the sharpest wounds, and those longest green, yield most freely the peaceable fruits of righteousness.'

'Such a blow as that would waken one up,' said Kate, gravely, after a few minutes' pause, during which she remained idly playing with the fringe of Miss Melville's shawl, while Grace had left the room with her key-basket, and Ernest and I had withdrawn to write letters in the little study which opened out of the breakfast-room. We could not help hearing the conversation which followed, though without any wish to play the part of eaves-droppers.

'What do you mean, Kate?' responded Miss Melville.

'I mean, that most people in this world seem to me to be asleep, or at least dreaming.'

'Are you sure you are awake yourself, my child?'

'No, I am not sure—in fact, I don't think I am. But I am as much awake as other people, I believe, even good people,' she added, as I knew, with one of those smiles whose wilfulness one always forgave for the sake of their exceeding beauty. 'I'm not good myself, and don't pretend to be; but those who are, mostly dream away their time much like the rest of us. They dream about different things, to be sure, but it is dreaming for all that. They are good in their own way, according to the bent of their natural characters; but they don't go *out* of their way to be good—they're not wide enough awake for that.'

'Again I must ask what you mean, my dear?'

'Why, I mean that if people are, for instance, naturally kind-hearted and helpful, they will go and work away among the poor, give them soup, and

blankets, and tracts, and so forth ; or, if they have a turn
for organising, they keep religious societies in motion,
and a great deal of useful machinery of that sort—all
very praiseworthy, you know.   I'm sure they're welcome
to do it if they like ; but then all the time, perhaps, they
are very cross, and selfish, and disagreeable, full of all
sorts of queer wrinkles, and angles, and roughnesses, and
yet they never think,'—

'Nay, nay, Kate, you are judging too hastily.   You
don't know how bitter may be the repentance which you
cannot see.'

'No ; but one should see the results of it, shouldn't
one ?' persisted Kate.   'Now, there's Miss Ellis ; she'll
go to the Sunday school in cloak and pattens through a
hail-storm, or tramp about in that filthy alley she calls
her district, till she's ready to drop ; and yet, if I make a
mistake in my copying, or if Helen isn't in to the minute
for tea, she's just as cross as can be.   All which proves,
as I said, that Christians are just as much asleep as the
rest of us ; for if they weren't—'

Here I lost the sense for a minute or two, being half
amused, half startled, and ashamed.   As for Ernest, he
wrote on with a gravity that was edifying to behold.
Whether he heard or not I could not tell.   But the next
words that fairly entered my understanding were from
Miss Melville.

'I'm afraid there is too much truth in it all, Kate ;
though still, dear child, should we not judge one another

more lightly, or rather refrain from judging at all? There are, as you say, many queer wrinkles and rough-nesses even in the best, which are unsightly enough, as we think, because we cannot look upon the hidden causes of which they are the result. We see the scar of a long-healed wound on the brow of a friend, and we turn from it, perhaps as the sign of defeat in some inglorious conflict; but it may be the token of victory—victory won at terrible cost—won where we should have fainted and fallen. The scar will always be there; but if we knew its history, we should wonder that it is not deeper.'

'Yes,' said Kate, with her ready candour; 'I suppose one often thinks that people are cross, when they are only sad.'

'And then, again, is it not true that those who are aiming high are more liable to faults and shortcomings than they who will be content with a sort of easy-going mediocrity? The noblest and highest things are most seldom seen in their perfect development. Weeds grow up and flourish year by year; but the corn and fruit for man's food, or the rare flower for his delight, are liable to be spoiled and blighted. But after all, Kate, we have nothing to do with others, except to be charit-able. Our great business is with ourselves; and if, as you say, *you* are not awake, my child, then there is a message for you here.' She turned over the Bible out of which Ernest had been reading at family worship, and pointed to Ephesians v. 4: 'Awake, thou that sleepest, and arise from the dead, and Christ shall give thee light.'

Kate read it aloud. 'Don't preach to me, Miss Melville, I get plenty of that ; Miss Ellis is always doing it. I sometimes think the little good there is in me will be lectured to death. But I shouldn't say such naughty things, should I ?' she added, with one of the sudden impulses which made her at once so attractive and so incomprehensible. 'Yet I do *think*, more and oftener than I seem to do. I'm *not* " only a humming bird," as Miss Ellis called me the other day.'

'Dear Kate,' said Miss Melville tenderly, and I could hear the soft sound of a kiss on the fair up-turned face, 'will you not only *think*, but pray ?'

'I must go to Helen,' was the hurried answer, and she rushed out of the room.

'That's a splendid piece of raw material,' said Miss Melville, when I joined her a few moments after.

'I wonder what it will be worked up into.'

'We must leave that to the Master, Elsie ; our clumsy, unskilful fingers would only spoil the work. Don't you think,' she added, gently referring, I felt sure, to Kate's remark about the lecturing, 'that we are sometimes a little apt to force our efforts to do good to others ?'

I took possession of the footstool which Kate had left, and looked up, as in happy days gone by, to the clear brown eyes which were always as soft as they were searching. It is so pleasant to be a child again now and then !

'I got a lesson just now, for I couldn't help hearing what you were talking about; and now I have come to confess that I have made some sad mistakes.'

'We all do that, Elsie, dear; but it's a great matter to find them out.'

'Well, I'm afraid I have not taken the right way with Kate. I have "preached" too much, as she says, as if I were standing myself on some superior height; or else I have petted and laughed at her, as one might pet a favourite kitten. Now, you treated her very differently. I should have been vexed with the child for speaking so strongly and hastily just now, and probably have tried to silence her with some severe reproof; while you reasoned with her, calmly and kindly, admitting the right of what she said, and yet showing her the wrong.'

'Perhaps it is easier for me to do this, than for you, dear;' and again came that soft touch upon my hair which I remembered of old. 'The young find it difficult to be patient with the mistakes of those who are yet younger, for they themselves feel the effect of them still too sharply and keenly; there is irritation even in the remembrance. But we stand further off. We have left the passionate intolerance of our earlier days behind, or ought to have done; and if only we have kept our sympathies fresh, we can bestow them even more readily than of yore. I recollect so well, so keenly still,' she added, 'the intense pain of being "sent back into myself," that I try to be very careful of inflicting it on another.'

There was a silence, during which I pondered, and, I hope, repented. It was certainly clear that I had been on a wrong track.

'Kate was right, Elsie,' said Miss Melville at length. 'I can see now—looking back from where I now stand, upon the mistakes of a life—that, as Christians, we don't sufficiently cultivate "whatsoever things are *lovely.*" We don't shine in the world with a *warm* light. It may be clear, though, alas! it isn't often that; but at any rate it's too generally cold. And then we *are* only half awake, as she says. Is not the old prophetic warning true for many Christians now: "Woe to them that are *at ease in Zion,*"—going on smoothly and dreamily with the world's badge in one hand, and the cross (as they think) held very loosely in the other? But it won't do. Elsie, my child, it won't do. Christ must have all, or we shall find, too late, that He will have none.'

.   .   .   .   .   .

How thankful we were for Miss Melville's presence in the dark days which followed; for no one could soothe the poor mourner as she could, saying not too much or too little, and saving us from the great mistake we were about to fall into, of attempting to comfort a sorrow which could not be comforted!

'Leave her alone; it is the truest kindness. There are times when even sympathy cannot be borne except

from Him, the unseen Helper. You may fix deeper the
dart which you are trying to draw.'

This was her parting charge to me, and I believe it
saved Helen from much which, to her reserved, reticent
nature, would have been absolute torture. How precious
is that rare gift of understanding, which seems especially
bestowed upon those who are God's ministers of comfort
in this sorrowful world!

Helen resumed her teaching when the Christmas
holidays were over. 'It was best for her,' she said, and
this we all felt it to be. So she went back meekly to
her work, leaving far behind the 'dim soft dusk of girlish
life;' but taking with her into her widowed womanhood
the presence of Him whose cry of agony on Calvary has
thrilled all time with its unutterable woe, and made Him
for ever the Comforter of the desolate, and the Healer of
the broken in heart.

XV.

HOW I MET AN OLD FRIEND.

'The bread of life is love ; the salt of life is work ; the sweetness of life, poetry ; the water of life, faith.'

—MRS JAMIESON'S *Commonplace Book of Facts and Fancies.*

CHAPTER XV.

HOW I MET AN OLD FRIEND.

SUPPOSE it is true that each day, while yet present with us, seems full of busy life and interest, full of struggles, and hopes, and fears, with comic, and, it may be, tragic touches here and there ; and yet it is curious into how small a corner of one's mind many such days may be rolled away, hidden, as it were, in the darkness of the past, and only lighted up, now and then, by a fitful gleam from memory's lamp.

But they are not lost to us, although they seem so. They are a part of us still. They have passed silently into the texture of our being, and though we cannot see now what part of its great design they have gone to fill up, we shall find it out by and by, when the whole lies unfolded before us in clearer light than this ; and then, perhaps, we shall see that the shaded neutral tints—the days which are neither joyous nor sad, but only flat—were as much needed as the dark or bright colours, which seem to us at present so much more worthy of notice.

. I need not chronicle here the daily minutiæ which need no chronicle. I remember only that hand and head were fully occupied, and both, now and then, a little weary. And yet I felt thankful that each had found its work, and that I was freed from the restlessness which had marred my peace in days gone by, when my energies had not found an outlet, and the outer and inner life were not yet in harmony.

Girlhood is often very bright, but as often, especially for those who think much and feel deeply, it is just the reverse, so that we need not grieve to exchange its restlessness and waywardness for the quiet strength of riper womanhood, with its power and content.

One Sunday evening, about twelve months after Ernest's marriage, I had gone as usual to the Church which we still attended together, and in which I shared a seat with the Hamiltons. It was some little distance from Wavertree, and we generally walked to and fro with the party from Claremont Terrace; but on this particular occasion, we set off alone, after waiting for them till we feared we should be late. I found afterwards that Kenneth had been suffering more than usual, and Grace had remained at home with him, while Ernest, contrary to his usual habit, had gone in another direction.

The service had already commenced when we entered

the Church. Surely I must have heard that voice somewhere before! I glanced towards the desk. Yes—it
was—it could be no other! And then I remembered
that our rector had recently engaged a new curate, whose
name I scarcely noticed when it was repeated to me—
the Rev. Edward Grey.

The sermon which followed was still from him, for,
on that evening, Mr Howard took no part of the service.
How well I remember it—the calm, unimpassioned de-
livery, the quiet voice, the pale, earnest face of the
preacher! It was not an eloquent sermon by any
means, and, so far as I remember, it was calculated to
make one rather uncomfortable than otherwise; not
soothing but searching; proclaiming, indeed, the Gospel
message of peace, but keeping not back its message of
warning.

The preacher's eyes fell once upon our pew, and I
knew that I, too, was remembered. I wondered whether
we should ever meet: but that did not seem likely. Mr
Grey could have no clue to my 'habitat,' nor would he
probably wish to ascertain it.

I speculated on this point for the space of two or
three hundred yards as I was walking home, and then
dismissed the subject as something worse than unprofitable. I might have had a dream once, perhaps, but I
had come to the conclusion that it was a very idle one.

And that night, as I caught a glimpse of myself in
the glass, while I removed my bonnet, it suddenly struck

me that I was growing old, or, if not old, at least decidedly middle-aged, and that the face of my youth had passed away for ever. Yes, there were deep lines under the eyes, and one or two upon the brow, and something which looked very like a streak of grey twining in and out among the bands of hair. Evidently it was time for me to cease dreaming.

I folded away the dress I had been wearing, and shut the drawer upon it with more emphasis and energy than the occasion at all demanded. But the action was typical; I was shutting a drawer in my heart at the same time. And yet, after all, I opened it again, and found, to my surprise, that there was more in it than I had thought. And the dying sweetness of old memories mingled with the freshness of new hopes; and I do not think the one could have been so deep and tender if it had not been for the other.

But there are some things one does not like to speak about, much less write. You may draw back the veil with your own hand from some secret corner of your heart, and gaze into it through tears that are not always sad: but you don't care to let other eyes peer in curiously, and note what they find there.

And so I will merely say that Edward Grey and I *did* meet, and that, in process of time, such a dash of sunlight fell at my feet, as made me almost question whether I had not wandered off my own path to one that belonged to somebody else. It seemed so strange that a lonely woman like me should find a home in a loving heart at last.

Not that Mr Grey by any means corresponded to my youthful picture of what my future husband might be. And very fortunate it was that he did not; for, if I had married my ideal, I am very sure I could not have lived with him, in addition to which, he would never have been likely to fancy *me*.

But God gave me something far better than I would have chosen for myself. He gave me a guide in my ignorance, and a strong stay in my weakness. He gave me one whom I could follow, even as he followed Christ. He gave me firmness which I should have feared, but for the almost more than womanly tenderness with which it was allied; and, linked with this, a wealth of that calm, and patient charity which believeth and hopeth all things. He gave me even more—the high privilege of ministering to one of His own labourers; of helping to bind the sheaves which another had reaped; and of following in the steps of the worker, to reach him, now and then, the cup of cold water, which even a weak hand may bring from the fountain.

And Edward never seems stern to me, however he may do so to others. I know he had many sorrows in his youth, and they have left their impress on the forehead, and have drawn some grave lines about the mouth; but the lines always relax by his own fireside, and his smile comes oftener there than anywhere else.

We had not a long engagement, for, very soon after our first meeting, Edward was presented to a living— not a very lucrative one certainly, but large enough, with his private means and my own small income, to justify us in getting married; so, at least, we thought—though we afterwards discovered that our calculation of household and incidental expenses was considerably below the mark. However, we were spared that weariful waiting, which, although it may draw closer the links of love and trust, does most certainly wear out certain other links, which hold an important place in our physical and mental economy.

Our new home, to my great delight, was in the mountain land already endeared by early association, not very far distant from Heatherstone either, for Mr Grey's cure was a small sea-port town on that same coast, beyond which I had often watched the sun sink down into the western sea. But I had never been to Deerfoot, and knew nothing either of place or people, save that the former was reputed to be dirty, and the latter as independent as they were hospitable.

Our wedding was very quiet. Ernest and Grace wished me to be married from their house, and would have spared no trouble or expense in the arrangements of the day. But we begged to be allowed to consult our own tastes in the matter, notwithstanding they were pronounced by all our friends to be not a little peculiar. We both felt that our marriage would be not the less solemn, but the more so, if our minds were left free from outward distraction, and fixed entirely upon the troth we plighted and the prayers we prayed.

So we drove quietly to Church one morning with Ernest and Grace, and were married without the help of either bridesmaid or groomsman. Ernest 'gave me away'—my faithful, loving brother,—and, as I laid my hand on my husband's arm, and felt it locked in the strong quiet clasp which promised as much as the words I had scarcely heard, I seemed to feel once more my father's hand upon my brow, and to hear the low tones of his murmured blessing. But another Voice had surely spoken, and a higher blessing I knew was ours—even His who had listened to our fervent prayer, that 'we might so live together in this life, that in the world to come we might obtain life everlasting.'

Our marriage tour was rather prolonged, for Edward wished to show me many parts of our beautiful country, to which I was still a stranger. But I soon grew very tired of this nomadic state of existence, and longed for the routine of settled duties, to which my husband mischievously insisted that I was more closely wedded than to him; but my half-expressed wish was eagerly seconded, and we travelled northwards as rapidly as possible.

It was evening when we reached our home—a calm, fair evening in early summer. The railway station was at some little distance from the parsonage, and a carriage was waiting to convey us thither. How beautiful the valley looked, with its fields and wood, and the mazy curves of its silver river! And though the smoke of the little town somewhat stained the clear sky at its further end, yet the sunshine rested there with its magic touch, powerful even in death, and transformed it into beauty. The air was full of dewy fragrance, and from the long low beach beyond the town came the moaning of the sea.

At length we turned in at the gate, and up the modest carriage drive, and Edward helped me to alight, and led me to the pretty drawing-room, newly furnished for my special welcome. And still, through the open window, came the breath of flowers and the music of the sea, and as we stood together, looking out into the soft purple twilight, my husband bent down to me and whispered—

'Can you be happy with me here, Elsie?'

Happy! Is the song-bird happy when the weary wings are folded at last in its sheltered nest? Is the storm-tossed sailor happy when he has reached the blessed haven, which is a faint picture of better things yet future? I gave him no answer, but I knew it was not needed. I leaned my head upon his arm, in such a fulness of rest, that even the softest speech would have jarred upon it, and our hearts mingled in the deep communion which is independent of words, as it is beyond their reach.

XVI.

SOCIAL WORK.

' What are we set on earth for? say, to toil,
  Nor seek to leave thy tending of the vines
  For all the heat o' the day till it declines,
  And death's mild curfew shall from work assoil,

—E. B. BROWNING.

CHAPTER XVI.

SOCIAL WORK.

THIS was the poetry of married life, but there-after came its prose. I was but just settled in my new home—had broken the prim order in which Mattie had disposed the drawing-room chairs, and gathered up the stray thoughts which her master allowed to float about the house in the shape of scraps of sermons, and notes of cottage lectures,—when I was overtaken by the tide of Deerfoot society, which came in its palest gloves and most resplendent bonnets, to express good wishes and eat bridecake. I am afraid Deerfoot was a little scandalized to find the bride in a brown holland apron and a pair of leather gloves, training the roses over the porch ; but still its welcome was very hearty, and the pure gold of kindly feeling shone not a whit the less fair, though its setting was somewhat of the homeliest.

Nevertheless I was not sorry when the congratulations were over, and the bridecake exhausted.

'Is it necessary for me to know all these people, Edward?' I asked, one evening, when our last visitors had departed.

'A serious question, Elsie,' said my husband, laying down his newspaper, and looking at me with an odd mixture of gravity and amusement in his face.

'It is—very,' I answered, speaking ruefully enough, I dare say, for there rose before my eyes a vision of a series of tea-drinkings which Deerfoot proposed to hold in my honour.

'What people do you mean, my dear? that we may clearly understand what we are talking about.'

'*Please*, Edward, don't call me "My dear," it's altogether too solemn. I sha'n't be able to say anything if you begin in that way. Well, I mean all who have called upon us—people of every shade of refinement and non-refinement.'

'Why do you object to them?'

One of Edward's direct questions, which are so trying, when no good answer is at hand. They cut sheer through a host of cobwebs, and bring one face to face with facts, and reasons, and troublesome matters of that kind, which it is sometimes convenient to forget.

'Oh, I don't *object* to any of them. They are very good and kind-hearted, I dare say ; but—'

'But what ?'

'They are not, as I said, particularly refined; some, I mean.'

'Not in manner or speech, I grant; but I think you may chance to find true refinement and delicacy of feeling when outward polish is none of the most brilliant. Besides, from this identical class are drawn my most regular Sunday-school teachers, and most active district visitors.'

I did not speak, being seized with a sudden interest in my sewing, and feeling, besides, ever so little perverse.

'You don't object to visit the poor, Elsie?' pursued my interrogator.

'Oh no; certainly not.'

'Yet they are not specially refined.'

'Hush, Edward. I was wrong, I see, and you have got a foolish little wife. Don't let us say anything more about it.'

'Nay, darling, let us rather talk the matter fairly over. And because my wife is not a foolish woman, but a sensible one, I wish her to consider it carefully. I have so often felt, Elsie, that, as Christians, we are apt to think too exclusively of the poor, and to neglect the claim of the classes above them—the respectable classes, entrenched behind certain bristling barriers, which are not to be passed or broken down. We know so little of the real *life* of these people. The icy, conventional crust that is over it seldom thaws to our touch. But there is work for us to do among them, if we will only set about it.   Their spiritual need is often great, and their spiritual destitution, I think, most appalling.'

'It's a difficult problem to deal with, isn't it, Edward?'

'Very,' was the reply, with a peculiar expression of those finely-chiselled lips, which I was at no loss to interpret; 'and difficult, for this reason among others, that many who will work bravely and self-denyingly among the absolutely poor, will not compromise their dignity by intercourse with those a grade or two below them in the social scale.'

'Well but, Edward,' I pleaded, clinging to my point with feminine pertinacity, 'it is pleasanter to mix in social intercourse with persons of refinement and education—now, isn't it?'

'Pleasanter, decidedly.   No one feels that more strongly than I do, and few can be more acutely sensitive to any jar upon taste or prejudice ; but, my dear wife—' and the grave eyes grew deeper in their meaning,—'we are not to think of pleasure only—our own pleasure. We know that our Master pleased not himself,—"came not to be ministered unto, but to minister,"—and we are told to please, not ourselves, but our neighbour, "for his good to edification."'

'Ah! provided it *is* "for edification."   But I don't think that is to be promoted by much visiting.'

'Not the visiting that ends in gossip and small talk, certainly.   But you know I do not ask for that ; and you know, too, how deeply I feel that this leaven of social dissipation spoils the force and freshness of our Christian life in these days. Nay, Elsie, we have need of a single eye and a right judgment in this, that we may only go where we can seek our Master's presence, and do our Master's work. But we know where to look for both, do we not?'

'And for sympathy, too?'

'And for sympathy too,—the *rest* from ourselves, and the power of soothing or strengthening another; the quick, loving intuition which perceives at once where our brother's burden presses, and the ready helpful hand to lighten it. We need all these in our social mission.'

'*I* need them. Oh, Edward, how blind I have been to many things!'

We were silent a long time then, while the twilight gathered slowly, and the stars came out one by one in the deep, dewy blue. Yet, far away in the west, there was still 'a light upon the shining sea,' that showed where the sun had set.

I soon learned to be very thankful that my husband had saved me from the great mistake of scrutinizing, too closely, the gradations of rank which existed in Deerfoot society. Very finely shaded they were, and not by any means so well defined as, in my innocence, I had imagined. Indeed, it was so difficult to comprehend their various and most minute ramifications, that at last I gave up the attempt in despair, and took refuge in my husband's often repeated maxim, that a clergyman should know no distinction of class, but should rather merge all in the sacred relation which subsists between a pastor and his people.

And, indeed, I found that the work which a wiser Hand appointed for me, day by day, lay precisely in the path which I had almost refused to follow. We received a kindly welcome from the poor, and had some friends among the rich; but those whom we seemed able to approach most closely, were neither the one nor the other.

'Elsie, have you seen the Miss Staceys lately?' asked my husband, one afternoon, meeting me in the principal street of our little town, as I was returning, rather wearied, from a visit to the school.

'No; but don't tell me to go to-day, Edward. I'm not up to the Miss Staceys; and, besides, I haven't time. There are fifty things I had planned to do at home.'

'Do forty-nine, then, darling, and make this visit the fiftieth. Poor Elsie! I'm afraid you are tired indeed; but if you could manage this one more call.—I found Miss Lucy very lonely and suffering yesterday, and her sister—well, goodbye; I'm off to a committee meeting.'

I turned my steps towards Baker Street, a little reluctantly, I fear, for I had promised myself a quiet rest on the sofa, and then, an uninterrupted time for some needlework, I was anxious to finish. I was very slow in learning that we are often not to do the thing we intend, but some other thing entirely different. And how much may depend upon our obeying or slighting the whispered hint which calls us off from our own precisely mapped-out plan of operations, to send us on some unexpected errand of duty for which we had left no space!

A few quick steps brought me to the Misses Stacey's door. They were the daughters of a former vicar of Deerfoot, much respected in the town and its neighbourhood, though I think held in some awe by the ladies, especially by young housekeepers like myself. Miss Lucy, indeed —a gentle, suffering invalid—was the last person in the world to be afraid of; but her elder sister, who seemed to think it her special mission to find out the wrong and set it right, was certainly somewhat to be dreaded.

Yes; Miss Lucy was at home, and would be glad to see me, replied the servant, in answer to my inquiry, and she ushered me forthwith into the back sitting-room, where the invalid was always to be found, propped up among her cushions, and generally occupied with some knitting, though, to-day, the shining wires were quiet, and industry had given place to pain. It was a pretty little room, opening upon a sheltered lawn, where golden leaves were falling fast and silently in the calm autumn sunshine, and a few late asters and chrysanthemums still remained to tell of brightness that had passed away. Miss Lucy welcomed me with her characteristic patient smile—a little more shadowed, perhaps, than usual.

'I'm afraid I can't talk to you,' she said, as she held out her hand; 'a violent fit of pain always leaves me feeling entirely exhausted. But my sister will be in soon.'

P

'Shall I read to you?' I asked, rather doubtfully; for, though Miss Nightingale had not then written her *Notes on Nursing*, I had already begun to suspect that if persons are too ill to read for themselves, they very seldom care to be read to. However, Miss Lucy, who did not suffer much from her head, welcomed the proposal, with eagerness.

'Something to rest me,' she whispered, in answer to my inquiry what she would like to hear; and, taking up an old well-worn book, which lay at hand, I read from it Baxter's well-known hymn:

> 'Lord, it belongs not to my care.'

She repeated with emphasis the last verse—

> 'Our knowledge of that life is small,
>   The eye of faith grows dim;
> But 'tis enough that Christ knows all,
>   And we shall be with Him.'

'I like that hymn so much for what it does *not* say. Descriptions of heaven are so wearisome. How one's mind turns away from them all to the Bible glimpses of it, which are so very fair, and pure, and satisfying: "And his servants shall serve Him; and they shall see his face."'

But just then there came a sort of rush through the house. It might have been the wind, but it was not; it was only Miss Stacey.

A handsome woman she must have been in her day, and very personable she was still, as I could not help thinking, when she opened the sitting-room door, and

came forward with a frank, kind greeting, and many·
assurances that I was precisely the person she was
wishing to see.

'For there are many things to be done, Mrs Grey,
and many arrangements to make. I really thought you
would have called upon us before,—I don't mean a *state*
call, you know, but just for a little friendly chat about
different matters. Things in the parish have been sadly
neglected—sadly; and now that we have got a lady at
the parsonage at last, we naturally expect—'

What Miss Stacey expected, she did not particularly
state; but her keen eyes surveyed me from head to foot
during this preamble, and I felt my face grow hot under
the scrutiny. I have no doubt that, in her own mind,
she had calculated the exact price of each separate
article of my dress, and decided whether or not it was
of proper material and colour, and suitable for what she
chose to call my 'position.'

'You see, my dear Mrs Grey,' she continued, throwing
off her shawl, and drawing towards her a large pile of
blue duffel petticoats, upon which she set vigorously to
work, 'your husband is a very good man, no doubt, but
still he only *is* a man.'

This being a fact which I could not well dispute,
though I did not exactly see its bearing, I waited in
silence for the oracle to declare itself further. Apparently
Miss Stacey considered that men were all very well in
their way, but in respect of administrative capacity, not

to be for a moment compared to woman, for she went on—

'And then Mr Rochney was a bachelor, too, poor man, and he couldn't do much ; so, of course, things got into a sad state.'

'What things, Miss Stacey ?' I ventured to inquire.

'Why, the Clothing Club, and the Mothers' Charity, and the Sick Fund, and all these.   It couldn't be helped ; what could he know about blankets and bags of baby linen ?   We did as well as we could, I and a few other ladies ; but we wanted a head sadly.'

'But, Miss Stacey,' I pleaded, much alarmed at the idea of being exalted as head over any working body, which boasted such an energetic, and, I feared, unruly member ; 'do, pray, let all these arrangements stand as they are.   I shall be most happy to give you any assistance in my power ; but I am very inexperienced, and have my hands tolerably full of home duties.'

'Of course, we know that,' said Miss Stacey, condescendingly.   'I told the ladies we must not expect too much, because you are only a beginner, and cannot have so much insight and tact in these matters as those who have grown old in the service ; but we shall all be willing to make allowances, I'm sure ; and if at any time I can help you by advice—   By the way, that reminds me, Mrs Grey, let me give you a hint not to patronize those Ratcliffes so much : it's best to keep people in their place.'

' I do not wish to patronize any one,' I answered ; 'I

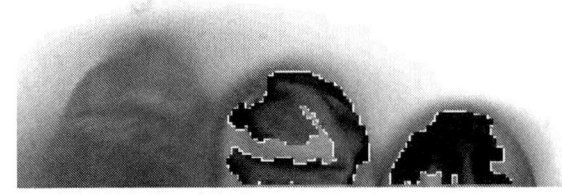

have such a great dislike to being patronized myself. I called upon the Ratcliffes, as upon the rest of my husband's parishioners, and in accordance with his wish.

But Miss Stacey was not to be thus silenced, and she went on to lay down the law as to my future proceedings with such energy and superiority, that my hot Irish blood was soon very nearly at the boiling point, and I made one or two sharp speeches, which certainly did not become 'my position,' either as clergyman's wife or Christian gentlewoman. However, I must do the good lady the justice to say that she was very forbearing with me, and we parted excellent friends. I fear Miss Lucy's pain was not improved by our discussion; but, after seeing thus much of her strong-minded sister, I no longer wondered that she herself hardly seemed to know whether she would like the blind drawn up or down, without a reference to 'Angelina.'

'Well, are you very tired, dear?' said my husband, meeting me at the gate on my return.

'I do think elderly unmarried women are the most—'

I stopped short, meeting the comical look upon his face, and remembering, to my confusion, that I had only been married about three months.

'Go and take off your bonnet, little wifie, and then come and have some tea.' Which I did, hoping my unfinished sentence would be forgotten. But as I was handing him his second cup, he inquired, 'if I had thought of an adjective?'

'An adjective?'

'Yes; you were in want of one just now to characterize a certain class, represented by Miss Stacey.'

'Oh! but you are naturally in a different state of mind before and after a meal which you greatly need; more just, perhaps, and certainly more charitable.'

'Well, perhaps Miss Stacey isn't a fair specimen.'

'I think not; though I wish there were more like her in her energy and practical knowledge.'

'But she interferes so dreadfully.'

'I must confess that. But don't you think it proceeds from this same energy, which has never yet found sufficient scope for its exercise? If she had been a poor man's wife, with a dozen children, or the head of a staff of hospital nurses, she would have recognised the principle of non-interference, and acted upon it. But her sister, and her maid, and the circle of Deerfoot charities, are altogether too small a field for her powers of organization, and so, from sheer necessity, she is compelled to use them, as she thinks, for the benefit of her neighbours; and if they are not grateful, they ought to be.'

'I'm afraid I am not.'

'I see you are not; but, you know, merit isn't always appreciated. There are substances whose property it is to promote a healthy irritation; but one doesn't feel exactly grateful to the irritant.'

I could not help laughing. 'Miss Stacey is irritating enough. I'm not very sure whether it's a healthy irritation.'

'Not if its *more* than enough. But seriously, Elsie, Miss Stacey's energy works wonders. She irritates, and agitates, and keeps up the funds of the different societies, as I don't think any one else could. She isn't over-refined, to be sure, or very remarkably comprehensive in her views; but her want of sensitive feeling helps her to carry her point where another would shrink. And it isn't always the many-sided people who are distinguished for firmness, or indeed for clearness either. Those who don't see far round them are apt to be sure of what they do see. And sometimes I think,' he added, musingly, 'that they possess a greater simplicity and *directness* of faith, which enables them more fully to give themselves up to God, and to walk with Him without doubt or question.'

'But the others have a nobler work, Edward; they are more tender in feeling and broader in sympathy.'

'They have each *their own* work, Elsie; and Miss Stacey, I am sure, has hers, for she is a true follower of her Lord, though His light within her has to struggle with some coarseness and ruggedness of the medium through which it shines.'

I fear I do not live so near the Master as Edward does, for I certainly have not the power of recognising His servants so readily. Alas! alas! how many who may be called to 'come up higher' by and by, we look down upon as far beneath us now.

I think it is Tholuck who speaks of the Christian

Church as a garden, in which are flowers of every hue, but all marked alike, as anemonies, which, though they may be crimson, or purple, or white, yet all bear the same dark mark by which they may be known. 'Even so the flowers in the garden of Christ are all marked by their heavenly Bridegroom, who has loved them even unto death, and signed them with His cross.'* Differences of character there may be, but the token of union with Jesus is always the same—His cross borne, and His cross rested in.

And do we not, in these days, need to hold fast this truth with special firmness? For there is a temptation, on the one hand, to be careless about 'the mark' if we find similarity of taste and temperament, or agreement in 'views;' and, on the other, to permit the want of these to separate us from many who, nevertheless, bear the true token, and, it may be, more clearly than we.

I do not mean to record here the details of our parish work, either in its success or its failure. There was plenty of the latter at first, for I, at least, made many mistakes, and entangled myself in divers perplexities, from sheer want of judgment. But I need not chronicle these, for I am only jotting down fragments of my life, and not following its whole course.

And, indeed, I must bring these jottings rapidly to a conclusion, having already scribbled much more than I

---

* Stunden christlicher Andacht.

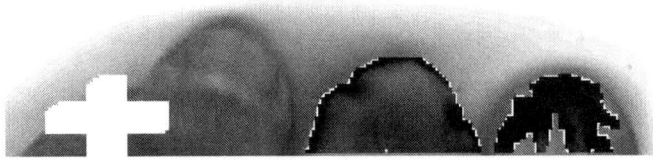

intended when I began. So I will 'skip,' as the children say, when they come to a page that looks what they call 'dry.' Not that these omitted pages were by any means dry to me. How fair, how very fair, they look even yet, and how much *more* fair they were then, when all that is now dead was glowing with the freshness of life!

And yet—and yet, I am sure that Edward and I are happier to-day than even in our earlier married years. There was a process of 'shaking together' to be gone through at first, which is vastly more pleasant in its results than it was in actual presence; especially since the willowy stage of existence was past for both of us, and we could not bend and intertwine quite so readily as we might once have done. I, at least, had been so accustomed to independence, both of thought and action, that it was a little difficult for me to learn to merge my will in another, and give up, even to my husband, what seemed to be my own. I think this lesson must be very hard, where true affection is not the teacher. Indeed, I often wonder how women *can* keep their promise to obey, when they have ceased to love and honour.

XVII.

DOMESTIC.

Mine be the reverent, waiting love,
  That waits all day on thee,
With the service of a watchful heart,
  Which no one else can see.
The love that in some hidden way
  No other eye may know,
Finds all its daily work prepared,
  And loves to have it so.

—A. J. WARING.

CHAPTER XVII.

DOMESTIC.

HERE are no little voices in Ernest's home. One baby-boy was with them for three short weeks, and then the Good Shepherd called him to the upper fold, where His lambs are for ever in His presence. Poor Grace! she was very sad for many weeks; but now she can give God thanks for the treasure He has taken into His own keeping.

For us, our 'olive branches' multiplied apace. Up-stairs and down-stairs I can hear the music of tiny feet, and often other sounds which are not musical at all. And from early morning, when the merry din begins, until the last curly head is laid upon its pillow at night, there is something for mamma to do—some lesson to teach, or some dispute to settle—or some baby grief to soothe; so that, if this history is rather disjointed and incoherent, reader, you must remember that it has been written under difficulties; for my only quiet time is after the children are in bed and before my husband has left his study,—a short space, often necessarily occupied with the needle rather than the pen, and always over when I hear his hand upon the door.

As to Grace, I thought, when I was staying with her in spring, that in many ways she was scarcely like a married woman. She seems so free and unencumbered, knowing little of the pressure of domestic and family cares. Of course, she has much time to herself during Ernest's daily absence, and she is able to keep up her writing, and to take part in many of the social and benevolent movements of the day; while I stay at home and teach my children, and mend their clothes, for, with Edward's small living, we cannot afford either governess or nurse.

I am often glad, indeed, to recollect that 'every member hath not the same office,' and while the gifted ones are fulfilling their higher calling, we 'ordinary women'—good, commonplace, serviceable wives and mothers, who know better how to love our husbands and children than to write about them—are not without our place or our use in God's world. In fact, on the whole, I do not think the routine of life could be carried on quite so comfortably without the help of the 'ordinary women.' Which is, at any rate, a satisfactory conclusion for me.

Yet, on the other hand, a wife should surely be some-

thing more than her husband's head nurse or house-keeper. A man has a right to expect some more intellectual entertainment at his fireside, than a mild hash of nursery small talk, seasoned with a dash of gossip. Yet not many recognise the duty of fitting themselves to give him anything better. It is true that we busy mothers have small leisure for mental culture. But I cannot help thinking we may do a good deal, indirectly, by simply keeping our minds awake and our ears open, and something too, directly, if we will only be energetic and methodical, and remember that time was given to be spent, not to be wasted.

It is surprising how many odd moments we may glean in the course of the day, by saving them from busy idleness. Which important lesson, however, I was myself marvellously slow to learn. I believe promptitude and punctuality are not naturally my strong points, however they may have been in some measure acquired; and certainly, in my early married days, the want of them introduced into our household various elements of discomfort and confusion.

'I can't think how it is,' I remember saying one day to Mary Wilton, who was paying us a visit, and who had been patiently waiting in the dining-room, with her bonnet on, an hour after the time I had myself appointed for a walk; 'I can't think how it is that this house seems always in a muddle. Now this morning, I am sorry to have kept you waiting, Mary, but I couldn't help it.

There are times when inanimate things seem to join in a conspiracy to vex one.'

Mary made no reply.   I am sure she knew very well where the fault lay.

'And, after all,' I went on, willing to justify myself, 'I sometimes think you very exact; orderly people are often in a kind of bondage; I question too, whether it is well to be always driving on at one thing after another— never stopping to take breath—leaving no spaces in one's life.'

'But there must be a medium somewhere; and because one thing is wrong, another is not consequently right.'

'No, no I don't mean that, and I am sure the want of punctuality often makes one have to drive far harder, and not overtake one's work after all.'

'I believe punctuality is the great remedy for muddle, Elsie,' said Mary, laughing, 'though I don't say it's the only one.'

'Well, what are the others?'

'Oh, there are several: faithfulness to one's self in little things, and a determination, as far as possible, to rule circumstances and not to be ruled by them.'

'Rather difficult, that last.   But what do you mean by " faithfulness to one's self?"'

'To one's own plans, and purposes, and resolutions, not allowing them to be broken through or set aside by impulse or indolence.'

'My dear Mary, all that is beautiful in theory, and worthy of a model single sister, as you are; but, in practice, it comes to pass that a thousand things beside impulse and indolence set one's plans aside. This morning, for instance, Edward was 'Mondayish'—had a nervous headache from yesterday's duty—required a darkened room, cold water applications, and various other little wifely attentions. Baby, meantime, was screaming himself into a fit in the nursery; cook was waiting orders for dinner; and Mr Wood was pacing up and down the study, wanting immediate advice in some parish difficulty, which advice I was to get from Edward, and convey to him as quickly as might be. Not one of all which things could I foresee or prevent. One can't help being ruled by circumstances.'

'Certainly, in one sense, that is true, but not in another. We needn't drift at the mercy of circumstances. There may be a thread of purpose running through every day, even though it doesn't always keep its place; and, at any rate, we may thoughtfully and prayerfully determine that habits of procrastination, or small forms of self-indulgence, or want of energy or method, shall be put down and overcome.'

'I suppose they are the authors of all the muddle, Mary,' I said, making for myself the application her politeness omitted. 'Well, I must think about it.'

And I remembered, to my confusion, that Mary's habits of quiet, orderly despatch—not of haste, for it was one of her maxims that time was never gained by being in a hurry—seemed to give her leisure both of heart and hand for any claim upon either; but I did not care to pursue the subject at that time.

'You are tired, Mary; let us sit down a while on this old tree-stump, which looks as if it had been laid here for your special convenience.'

'Why can't Miss Wilton walk as far as you, mamma?' asked little Willie, who was with us, coming up with his hands full of daisies, the search for which had kept him thus far unwontedly quiet.

'Because she isn't so strong as mamma, Willie,' said Mary, lifting the child on her knee, and proceeding to make a chain of the daisies, after the fashion which has delighted children from time immemorial. There was a curious contrast between the two faces—one so round and rosy, glowing with happiness and health; the other with pain as well as patience stamped on brow and lip, and endurance as well as peace looking out from the quiet eyes; for Mary was almost entirely an invalid now, with little hope of being ever restored to ordinary health.

Willie's thoughts were apparently running on something else than daisies. 'Why can't you walk like mamma?' he persisted, lifting his blue eyes to her face.

'Because I have a great deal of pain, dear Willie.'

'Who gives it you?' asked the child, with an earnest gravity, that very nearly upset mine.

'God,' said Mary, in a low, reverent voice.

'Why?' He was such an inveterate little reasoner, that if he once got hold of a subject, he was never satisfied until he had pursued it to the end.

'To make me patient, Willie, I suppose.'

'Couldn't He make you patient without pain?' asked Willie, unconsciously striking upon a difficulty over which older heads and hearts have ached and pondered for ages.

'He *could*, Willie, but He sees it better not; and God knows best, my child, always remember that. Now go and bring me some more daisies.'

'What curious things children are!' said Mary, when the little catechiser was out of hearing, 'and how fearlessly they bring out into open daylight questions which we keep hidden in dark corners of our mind!'

'Yes; I should think you must often have wondered whether God couldn't make you patient without pain.'

Her lips quivered for a moment, then fell into their old quiet lines again. 'It's a great comfort to know that the sharp instrument is held in a loving hand. But yours is the wider life now, Elsie—do you remember our old talks about this?—and mine seems so—so *broken off* and incomplete. Formerly I used to be able to feel, every evening, that something had been *done* during the day —that some tangible result remained from the hours of waking thought and activity; but now my days are like blank spaces, and I haven't energy to fill them up.'

'Don't you think that the best and highest results are just those which are not tangible, those which we cannot weigh, and measure, and appreciate by any power of calculation we possess at present? And I can't help feeling we make great mistakes in this matter. It isn't so much what we *do*, but what we *are*—the struggle with self and sin, and the victory gained by the power of Christ. God looks at these things with larger, other eyes than ours ; and it may be that the very days which seem to us like blank spaces, are in His sight full of the "peaceable fruits of righteousness;" for He can see that, though we may have done little, we have endured much.'

'If one could be sure of that! But the patience which dear Willie talks about seems often so far off.'

'Ah! but Mary, must we not have patience with our *want* of patience? It will have its perfect work; but that must be in God's time, not ours.'

'Thank you, Elsie; you always think of exactly what I forget.'

'And *vice versa*, isn't it? I think we balance one another nearly as well as we used to do in those never-ending talks under the lime-trees at Retford. Do you remember?'

'Do I not? I can hear the bees among them at this moment. Ah! Elsie, new friendships are very precious; but somehow they seem to lack the savour of the old. I don't seem thoroughly at home with anybody unless I can say, "Do you remember?"'

'There's another thing, Mary,' I said, hardly heeding the past in the new thought of the present ; 'may there not be some whose work it is just to be quiet—little bits of stillness in this restless world ? We busy people are apt to be so much absorbed in our work that—'

'Better than being absorbed in *yourselves*, Elsie, which is a danger I often feel to be very real. Ah ! there are slippery places in every path ; but surely "He knoweth the way that we take !" He knows, and He will keep.'

'He knoweth !' Ah ! how much need I had to remind myself of that truth, before many hours were over !

'Come with me and look at the babies,' I said to Mary that night, when we had left Edward to study his sermon in quiet. He looked up, with the nearest approach to a mischievous smile of which he was ever guilty.

'Elsie performs an act of baby-worship every night, Miss Wilton ; don't you go and encourage her in it.'

'Hush ! Edward ; as if you didn't do the same thing yourself ; yet,' I added, as we went upstairs, 'I do pray that I may not idolize them—may remember that they are *only lent*. But no one knows how those tiny fingers do twine about one's heartstrings.'

We went into the night nursery. Only Bertie and Willie were here, for Helen, at her special request, had been promoted to the honour of sleeping with Miss Wilton ; and little Gracie still occupied her pink-lined cot in our room, whence, every morning, she crept to her papa's side, and laid her bright little head on his shoulder. But Willie was not asleep. He was sitting up in his crib, looking flushed and feverish.

'Willie, my boy, are those little eyes of yours open still? Why are you not asleep?'

'God wants to make Willie patient,' said the child, looking at us with a dreamy, half-bewildered expression.

'What is the matter, darling?'

He threw himself down on his pillow, murmuring—oh! words of terrible omen to a mother's heart—'Willie's head.'

I took him up, and held him for a moment in my arms. His little hands were burning, and his breath was hot and feverish. He complained of his throat, too, and asked eagerly for a drink. Mary's eyes rested on mine for a single second; but neither of us gave utterance to the dread which was in our thoughts. I put the child back in his crib, and told Mary to ask my husband to go for a doctor.

He came, and my worst fears were realized. 'Scarlet,' was the one word he uttered, after a brief examination of his little patient.

'But keep up your heart, Mrs Grey,' he added, as he followed me into another room; 'there's no reason why the child shouldn't do well enough. We'll bring him through, I hope, bravely. Keep the other children away, and don't be too anxious yourself. Good-night; I'll look in early to-morrow.'

He was a kind-hearted man, though noisy and rough withal, and not over-refined ; but still there was a degree of comfort in his brisk, firm step, and the ring of his cheery voice. I repeated over and over to myself the assurance that there was no need for anxiety. They were only words, to be sure ; but do we not all know how much such words will contrive to yield, with hard pressure, when we are determined to extract all they will give ?

Yet when Mr Bennett came the next morning, I fancied he looked grave. Edward had been summoned suddenly to visit a dying parishioner ; and, leaving Mary for a moment by Willie's bedside—for she had promised not to forsake me in my trouble, but to stay and help in nursing, as far as strength permitted—I followed him down to the study.

'Doctor, is it a serious case ? You don't think—' I stopped, for the words choked me.

'Scarlet fever is always serious, more or less,' was the oracular response ; and I could get no other, for the good man worked himself unto his overcoat, and hurried away.

I lingered for a moment before going upstairs, and threw myself on my knees beside Edward's table, hardly to pray—for the tumult of feeling seemed to have carried me beyond that—but to lay my fear in silence before Him who could read it all, and who would surely pity as a father pitieth his children. Something of this thought came into my mind as I knelt, with a soft breathing of peace, but I could scarcely grasp it yet. There was comfort, however, in the mute posture of appeal, and I arose stronger.

It was the first cloud in the fair sky of our wedded life, and, like the disciples of old, we feared as we entered into it ; but faith could behold, even then, the brightness of its golden lining, and rest in the love which shone on the other side.

But I will not dwell on the long agony of the week which followed : how, at every visit, the doctor's face looked graver and more anxious ; how hope grew fainter and more faint, until at length it died out into the white ashes of despair ; how at length the fever passed, and the restlessness of delirium was stilled, and the precious little life ebbed quietly away, while a solemn stillness fell upon the house, and in silence we watched and waited for the unbidden guest whose coming we knew was near.

It was the evening of a calm September day— September, with its flowers, and fruits, and gathered sheaves. The sunset light had faded upon the sea, and given place to the greyness and chill of approaching night. Through the open window came the low, wild wailing of the waves, as they broke upon the shore ; but this was the only sound we heard, as we sat together— my husband, and Mary, and I—except our darling's laboured breathing as he slept. We did not speak— there were no words for an hour like this, when even thought is overborne by intensity of feeling,—but in the silence we could almost hear the music of that far-off land, where the shining ones stand before the throne.

The blue eyes opened at last. 'No pain now; but God can make Willie patient,' he murmured, still going back to the thought which had run, like a silver thread, through all his wandering. 'I can say my text, mamma: "He shall gather the lambs"—' But it was never finished here; perhaps the angels heard it as they carried him beyond the river.

A kind of *hush* fell upon us all after Willie was taken. The other children seemed quieter in their play, as if even they missed the ringing voice and gleeful laugh which we thall never hear again.

'God has had Willie a long time now,' I heard Helen whispering to herself one morning, as she sat among her toys on the nursery floor; 'I wish He would let him come back and play with Helen. Not his soul,' she added, correcting herself with curious gravity; 'Helen wants Willie's body that he used to have—Helen doesn't like souls.'

I wondered what the childish vision of a soul might be, or in what world of dim imaginings she had picked up her idea, that 'Helen didn't like souls!'

But still our home has grown more sacred,—nearer, as it seems to me, to that other home which our boy has reached before us. And for myself, I am sure I needed to have my steps quickened thither, and my eyes unsealed to a clearer vision of its glory. For I had grown too careful, too earthly; oppressed and harassed by many duties, or what I fancied were such. There were home claims first—always imperative, and often almost overwhelming; for, as I have said, our income was limited, and much personal effort, as well as thought, was needed on the part of the house-mother,' to solve the difficult problem of 'making ends meet.'

And beyond these were parish claims, which Miss Stacey was constantly pressing upon my attention, reminding me of the duties of my 'position,' and the expectations formed of a clergyman's wife.

'I do not see why they should be so very excessive, Miss Stacey,' I pleaded at first; 'most ladies, whose income is not unlimited, find the care of their household and children a sufficient tax upon their energies. Why should my work begin where that of my neighbour ends? I did not share my husband's ordination vows.'

But my mentor was inexorable. She laboured hard herself, and she had no idea of sparing others; so she drew me on from one thing to another, till I had as much to do as would have given full employment to an energetic deaconess. It was a very busy life, and I soon found that it was not quite a healthy one. The strain upon mind and body was too great for both, and I think, in its measure, the spirit suffered as well. There is such a thing as working, even in God's service, beyond our measure; giving more than we are receiving, spending ourselves in outward effort, while we forget to maintain the freshness of our own communion.

'But I do not see what I can do less,' I appealed to my husband one day, after this idea had slowly dawned upon my mind. 'You and Mr Wood have already as much on your hands as you can manage; and, after all, there are certain delicate springs which a woman's fingers can touch better than yours.'

'That is true, dearest; but this other is a truth also —I leave the application of it to yourself,—that we may become so absorbed in our work as to be forgetful of our Master; and yet, unless we are looking up to Him in it all, so as to catch His smile and receive His strength, we may be in reality doing very little, while we seem to be doing a great deal.'

'Then the remedy here would be, not to work less, but to pray more.'

'Certainly; was it not Luther who said that now he had so much to do, he was obliged to spend three hours a day in prayer?'

'But, Edward, I do not feel that I *can* do all I am attempting at present. I get worried and worn, and cross, and I haven't time for quiet thought.'

'My poor Elsie, then it's no wonder you feel worn and worried! If you have not time to be alone with God, you are surely doing too much—doing what He has not given you. It is only they who wait upon Him, remember, who " renew their strength."'

'Ah! but it is not really possible for me to get the quiet hours I used to have before I married. However, I suppose one may touch the hem of Christ's garment, even in the crowd of daily duties and cares. But about my parish work, how can I give anything up? What will Miss Stacey say?'

'Never mind Miss Stacey! She's a very good woman; but you needn't make a pope of her. We Protestants are rather given to setting up many popes instead of one, and surrendering our right of private judgment to them, too.'

'But people will think—'

'Why should you trouble yourself about what people think? My dear wife, I believe that is one of Satan's most subtle snares.'

'I don't, in general.'

'But you do in particular. We don't care for *the world*; it's an abstraction we can't realize. But we do care for certain individuals in it; and especially we care for the Christian world, so called. We value its approval, and deprecate its condemnation. But we have to learn, Elsie—and I sometimes think it's one of the most painful lessons of life, as well as one of the most useful when it *is* learned—to stand alone, even from that. To our own Master we stand or fall; and we must not heed so much the voices of our fellow-servants. "*Study to show thyself approved unto God.*"'

'Then you think—. What would you advise me to do, Edward?'

'Nay, Elsie, I cannot advise; but there is one question which is always sure of an answer: "Lord, what wilt *Thou* have me to do?" He will show you, if you ask Him, though it may be by some secret teaching, which is clear to your own eye alone.'

But still I went on, restless and busy, crowding more work, rather than less, into the days that were overcrowded already, until Willie's death made a lull in my life, and, in the stillness which it brought, I learned at last a lesson I had dreamed before—*the* lesson, I think, which ensures to us power and success in our work for the Master—that it is only when we are *prepared* for our work, by living in secret with God, that our labour is not in vain. The words we speak must be learned fresh from the lips of Christ, and then spoken from the depths of our own heart, or they will fall powerless, though in themselves they may be good and true.

XVIII.

'FROM A WILD CAT TO A KATE.'

'To thine own self be true.'

—SHAKESPEARE.

CHAPTER XVIII.

'FROM A WILD CAT TO A KATE.'

Y dear Miss Melville, don't lecture me; please don't! I haven't learned to like it any better than I did, in the old time, at Wavertree.'

That ringing voice! It could be no other than Kate Hamilton's. And Kate, to be sure, it was, with her peerless face and queenly step, just entering the Parsonage drawing-room through the low window which opened on the lawn, and bringing with her the freshness of flowers and sunshine in one. And that was Miss Melville; for we had tempted her once more—for the last time, as it proved—from her quiet mountain home, and she was holding my little daughter Helen entranced with the identical stories which had delighted my own childhood. .

But how came Kate to Deerfoot? Not as a visitor,

for she and her sister Helen were at the Parsonage only
for the day, but as a resident in the quaint old house
which stood midway between us and the town, nestling
among shrubs, and half grown over with ivy.   Not
because Helen had realised a fortune by teaching, or
Kate by law-copying; but because the 'uncle in India'
did not, in this case, prove a myth, but a substantial
reality, who, having lived and died in single blessed-
ness, left some twenty thousand pounds to be divided
among his nearest of kin.

And as Helen and Kate were the only two persons
who could make good their claim to this title, they
became sole heirs to the bachelor John Hamilton's
hoarded riches; and, after travelling for a year, they had
finally settled at Deerfoot,—at least Helen had, for Kate
could scarcely be said to settle anywhere; but she made
it her headquarters, and considered it nominally her home.

Absolute freedom and uncontrolled wealth had not
exactly improved Kate.   She had grown more wilful
than ever; somewhat given to manias, and a good deal
to flirtation; but very loveable still, and with the same
undefinable charm about her as of old.   At present it
was her pleasure to be decidedly 'fast'—the first specimen of the genus 'fast young lady' which had presented
itself before the astonished eyes of this respectable and
rather sleepy little borough, which was a good deal
puzzled by the unusual phenomenon, and disposed to
regard it as something 'no canny.'

In fact, she persisted in doing such extraordinary things, and giving so much employment to gossipping tongues, that her sister grew seriously annoyed and uneasy; and, after remonstrating in vain herself, requested me to try if I could not bring her back to more sober ways. But I suggested that Miss Melville, to whose influence Kate was much more likely to defer, would accomplish the task better than I; so I gave her a hint of the state of matters, and left her to do as she thought best. She had been with us for some little time, hearing and seeing, though not seeming to notice, the young lady's extravagances, and entering into all her pursuits and plans with a freshness of interest which never wearied, before she ventured a very gentle but decided disapproval of a wild frolic perpetrated by certain Liverpool girls of her acquaintance, which Kate, with a mixture of fun and daring, had just retailed for our benefit.

It was in answer to this that Kate had put in her plea against lecturing, stepping into the room,—for she had been standing outside the window,—and coming round to the back of Miss Melville's easy-chair. The latter drew off her spectacles, and looked up into the glowing face which hung over her.

'Nay, Kate, I'm not fond of lecturing any more than you of being lectured. I was merely expressing an opinion; and I cannot think that smoking cigarettes, as you call them—though what these may be I do not pretend to know,—and riding over hedge and ditch in that reckless, break-neck fashion, are at all elegant or feminine proceedings.'

'Well, perhaps it *was* a little fast,' replied Kate, 'which I know is very shocking to some delicate sensibilities. But fast young ladies are not of entirely modern growth, Miss Melville ; they must have existed in all ages. I believe there were some among the maidens who helped Penelope to spin that everlasting yarn, which "did but fill Ithaca with moths." Indeed,' added the saucy child, without waiting for a reply, 'I strongly suspect that all and sundry who now so dolefully bewail the degeneracy of modern womankind, were, in their younger days, a little, just a very little, fast themselves ! They don't give any hint of it, you know : but if you ever hear two very proper elderly ladies fighting their battles o'er again, there are various unconscious revelations which lead one to infer—'

She stopped, and finished her sentence by an indescribable arching of her eyebrows.

'Kate, Kate,' laughed Helen, who had come into the room in time to hear this last sentence; 'what an incorrigible child you are ? I hope Miss Melville won't forgive your impertinence.'

'She will,' said Kate, securely, 'Miss Melville is always indulgent to truth, however unpalatable; and in the present instance—'

'In the present instance,' said the dear old lady,

assuming the gentle air of command which always subdued Kate's lawlessness, 'it seems to me that the fast young lady of this present day is of a different type from anything that I remember. It is not only that the exuberance of health and youthful energy is as uncontrollable as ever, and as little to be restrained by conventional manners and maxims; but it displays itself in a new form—new and not pleasing. This fastness is something from which, I think, every instinct of true womanhood involuntarily shrinks—something which men themselves most certainly despise; however they may choose, some of them, to flirt with it, and be amused at it.'

'Dear me!' said Kate, looking up with an expression of mock dismay; 'that unfortunate remark of mine was like pulling the string of a shower-bath! But aren't you just a little severe?' she added, more gravely. 'I know many fast girls who are very—I mean, there's no harm in them.'

'I fully believe that, dear—most fully. Their womanliness is there, as true and pure as ever, I know; but then it has lost the fresh, dewy sweetness which was its greatest charm. The lily may be a lily still; but if it *will* peer adventurously above the broad, cool shadow of its sheltering leaves, its early fragrance and purity must be marred. And we cannot afford,' she added, while her eyes· kindled again with something of their old brilliance, 'to let the ideal of womanhood be lowered in these days. The tendency of the age is not to an excess of deference, either towards the weak or the sacred.'

'People make very unkind remarks sometimes, I know,' said Kate, tapping the floor impatiently with her foot, and getting rather angry, as she felt herself coming to the worse.

'No doubt they do—remarks which are not worth minding. But still we are not called upon to bid needless defiance to the habits and maxims, which English society has laid down as to a woman's position and conduct.'

'But they are only conventional; and, I'm sure, they are very often over-strained.'

'That may be; but still, when a woman dares to set them lightly aside, from mere recklessness or love of singularity, she is placing herself, to say the least, in a very invidious position. If the path of duty seems to run counter to them, then let her go bravely forward, and trust in God's shielding; but she ought to be very sure of that.'

'But you don't like women to be dependent and helpless, Miss Melville,' pleaded Kate; 'and I'm sure I know ladies who are afraid of doing anything for themselves, lest they should be thought masculine.'

'Then they are very silly, Kate. Womanliness is not a synonym for usefulness; and Mrs Grey knows it has long been my doctrine that a woman should not only be able to take care of herself in all the minor emergencies of life—'

'Not lose half her luggage at a railway station, for instance,' put in Kate, by way of illustration.

'Exactly, my dear; but that, also, if she chooses to earn her daily bread by work in which the world is not yet accustomed to see a woman's fingers employed, rather than in a strictly feminine occupation for which she has no taste, nobody has any right to blame her.'

'Women are asking a great deal now,' said Kate, glad, I think, to turn the subject.

'Ay, they are. They are making higher claims than women ever made before, or ever dreamt of, in my younger days—I don't say whether wisely or not. But, at any rate, if they do make such requests, they ought to support them worthily; and whimsical extravagances and peculiarities are not likely to gain for them either patient hearing or candid consideration. They should show themselves both worth hearing and worthy of being heard, or their cry will be put down as the mere babble of foolish children, who must be taught wisdom by rebuke.'

A silence of some minutes, broken at last by Kate—

'What are we to do, after all, Miss Melville? How are we to know when we are right in these things, and when we are wrong?'

'Let us be true to ourselves, my child, to our own womanly instincts. It is when we are false to these, though it may be in some apparent trifle, that we get on debateable ground. God has implanted them, and God will guide us in their interpretation. He will lead us,' she added, laying her wrinkled hand fondly on the girl's shoulder, as she knelt before her—'He will lead us in every doubtful path, and strengthen us in every rough one, if we will only learn, even in trifles, to study and love His will. For, after all, Katie dear, we can only reach the highest ideal of womanhood by aiming at the highest standard of holiness.'

'I am often discouraged about Kate,' said Helen, sadly, when the former had left the room.

'Why should you, my dear? Can we not trust our Father to bring the wanderers home, even from a "far country," perhaps by a way which *we* know not, but which He can see to be the only one to draw them into communion with himself?'

'Yes; but she is so volatile, so indifferent. She gives no sign of interest in heavenly things.'

'Ah! my child, God works more slowly than we. We want the seed to spring up and bear fruit in a day; but the silent dew must fall upon it first, and winter's frost and summer's heat must do their part as well. We must have patience and faith. And then hers is so truly a childlike nature,' she added; 'and for such there is always double cause for hopefulness. Those who are willing to be led, will never fail of a guide.'

.   .   .   .   .

'Who is that young lady in a sort of cloudy white

dress? She was speaking to our hostess a minute ago; but now I've lost her. Oh! there she is again—a girl with a coronet of dark hair.'

'That? That is Kate Hamilton. She *is* very lovely, is she not?' But the speaker was too much riveted to answer me.

It was the day following that morning talk which I have already recorded. Miss Hamilton was returning the civilities of Deerfoot by a small dinner and evening party, and my husband and I were invited, as a matter of course. How changed she was from the Helen of our earlier acquaintance! I could scarcely believe her the same, as I watched her moving among her guests, pale and calm as ever, but a trifle stately now, and the least bit in the world peculiar. Yes, she was, there was no denying it; and yet she was very dear. Not a girl now, but a middle-aged woman, so she seemed; appearing, in her still, grave composure, older than she really was.

She looked well to-night, in her rich black velvet, relieved by a narrow frill of Valenciennes. And I suppose not many would have guessed the history which lay hidden away in the depths of those soft eyes, whose mournful light told, now and then, of the flowing of an inner current that would always be out of sight. But, though Helen never spoke of her sorrow, I knew it was with her still. Years had softened, but not healed it. Nothing could do that, except the leaves of the tree of life.

'The name of Hamilton is curiously familiar to me,' said Kate's unknown admirer, Captain Raeburn. He was staying at Deerfoot Hall, and had accompanied Mr and Mrs Charteris, as their visitor,—an uninvited guest, whom Helen had welcomed with her usual self-possessed courtesy. He and I happened to be standing together, a little apart from the rest, in a position to overlook the whole room with its various groups. Sufficiently commonplace they might seem to a commonplace observer; but an educated eye and ear could find in each the materials of a picture, and hear from all the 'still, sad music of humanity,' with its strange discords and harmonies, its sobs of unsatisfied longing, and its wail of passionate regret. And, on the whole, it was a pretty scene,—almost picturesque, in spite of nineteenth century absurdities.

But, perhaps, I should be expected to make some reply to my companion; so I ventured a remark to the effect that the links of association were very subtle, and not always easy to trace.

'But I can trace this, or I think I can. Do you know the lady's Christian name?—Helen, is it Helen?'

'Yes,' I replied, a little wondering.

'Ah! then, I remember I was coming home from the Mauritius—a few years ago now—been out there on account of health,—and in the same packet there was a young clergyman, with whom I became rather intimate. Poor fellow! he was taken ill—died, in fact, of fever; but in his delirium he was continually asking for Helen, and once he called her " Helen Hamilton." Can it be—'

He stopped abruptly; for we both caught sight of a figure, with slow step, and white, rigid face, gliding noiselessly through the door near which we stood. Captain Raeburn looked shocked. No doubt about indentity now!

'How very unfortunate! I had no idea Miss Hamilton was so near. Dear, dear, what could I be thinking of!'

And the poor man's self-reproach was so extreme, that though feeling for Helen more than I could tell, I was fain to make the best of it, and comfort him as well as I could.

'What would you advise me to do, Mrs Grey?' he asked in his distress.

'Nothing, certainly—nothing. Anything you can do will only make things worse.'

For Helen was not one to suffer even a friend to speak of her past, much less a stranger.

But in a few moments she returned, the sharp agony over, and no trace of it remaining, except a look of sorrowful patience. And she walked straight up to Captain Raeburn, and entered at once into conversation with him about the season and the country, partly, perhaps, to set him at ease; partly, with a woman's pride, to show that she was no longer weak.

But, as they talked, there came from the adjoining room the wild wail of that most mournful song—

'Home they brought her warrior dead.'

And I knew that Helen heard it, for she shivered slightly, and turned pale.

XIX.

CONCLUSION.

'She was like
A tender neutral tint, that blent all hues
And harmonized them,—good to rest upon
For eye and heart.   Her life had all been given,
To filling up the many blank of love
Around her : claiming none, all claimed of her,
And, fed from some full, deeply hidden spring,
Her pure true sympathy unfailing flowed.'

—ISA CRAIG.

CHAPTER XIX.

CONCLUSION.

 NEVER, after this visit, saw my dear old friend Miss Melville again. She died very soon after her return to Heatherstone— passing peacefully away from the solitude of her earthly home, to the presence of the Lord she loved. In the midnight watches He came to her, and found her waiting; and now I know that she sees His face, and is at rest.

And thus the last link was broken to my early home. I look back now and then to all the old life there, with even yet a little sigh of regret that it can never return. For though a new life may come, deeper, richer, fuller than the past, yet the old one comes again no more, and that which has for ever gone from us is for ever sacred.

But such retrospect is neither wise nor healthy. Far better to be pressing towards the mark, 'forgetting the things that are behind, and reaching forth to those which are before.' And, after all, I am often thankful that the past is past, and can never, by any possibility, be turned into the future; thankful that the turmoil and unrest of the earlier voyage are over, and that I am drawing nearer, day by day, to fair haven and safe anchorage.

About this time a curious change came over Kate Hamilton. Whether from the remembrance of Miss Melville's admonitions, or from some other unexplained and unexplainable cause, I cannot say, but she certainly laid aside all her extravagances, adopted an odd pre-Raphaelite style of dress, and astonished my husband by requesting the charge of a visiting district, and a class in the Sunday school.

'Perhaps I ought to have refused her,' he said to me afterwards; 'she will do no good—she is working *for* life and not *from* life.'

'But may she not *get* good, Edward? Are not teaching and being taught only different stages of the same lesson?'

'It may be so; but, Elsie, it's a terrible thing to be deceived with the idea that we are serving God when we are only serving self, worshipping the same idol under another name, and that the holiest. I believe Satan ruins many through this snare. They are among the vineyard labourers, and so they take for granted that all must be well; but they don't stop to inquire whether they are themselves grafted by faith into the living Vine.'

It was not, however, in Kate's nature to continue for any length of time steadily plodding on in the same track. She could not help making erratic darts hither and thither, upsetting all the theories one might have been at the pains to form about her; so I was not greatly surprised when she announced one day that she was 'tired of poking about in dirty cottages, inhaling un-savoury odours, and talking to people that didn't care to listen.' She wanted some variety, and meant to get up a pic-nic party to Combe Point, a craggy spot upon the shore, a mile or two from Deerfoot.

'Not a grand pic-nic, Mr Grey, involving champagne and stupidity. We'll go down some afternoon, and boil the kettle gipsy fashion, and have an early tea among the rocks, and improve our knowledge of the marine flora, as one of your neighbours calls it; in other words, we'll potter about for seaweed, and catch crabs and enjoy-ment.'

'I hope that last item will not be so doubtful as the crabs, Miss Kate; but if you can persuade the mother to leave her babies, we will come.'

'She needn't; let the babies come too. Elsie would only be half there without them—her mother wings would be in a continual flutter, for she can't settle down quietly and rationally anywhere unless the nestlings are near.'

s

So it was arranged, and on the day appointed we repaired to the place of rendezvous, where we found assembled a large and somewhat curiously-assorted party; for Kate seemed to have exercised her ingenuity in gathering together as strange a mixture of social materials as could well be devised. However, the gipsy tea, and the babies, and the necessity for scrambling among the rocks, soon brought us all into harmony, and our search for enjoyment was as successful as Kate herself could desire.

It was, in truth, a very pretty scene. The sunlight was glittering everywhere—on the white sails which gleamed in the distance; on the anchored boats which rocked on the coming tide; on the wet strips of sand; and on the crisp, curling waves which broke with a low sweet murmur upon the shore. The sky was blue and clear, except that round the horizon were gathered piles of snowy clouds, which one could almost fancy the outer ramparts of that city where the redeemed shall walk in white. How good it is that God has given us, even on earth, so much to remind us of the unseen glory!

'I don't think my district work prospers much, Mr Grey,' I heard Kate say, as, in the course of her rapid flitting from group to group, she stopped for a moment beside the rocky pool where Edward was showing the children the home of the limpets and the seaweed. There was an eager, wistful look upon her face, which I had often noticed of late, the token of some mental unrest which she would not acknowledge. I turned aside, and occupied myself in helping Helen and Bertie to build their sand-castle; but still I could not avoid hearing her say—

'I shall resign my office, I think, and the Sunday school teaching too. I don't feel as if these things were much in my line. I can't imagine how people go on doing good, or trying to do it, year after year, without being awfully tired.'

Edward did not reply for a moment. I think he saw that her words were lighter than her thought.

'And yet,' she added, half regretfully, 'it must be very pleasant to be of some use in the world. I do sometimes wish I could live to any purpose.'

'Is there not something to be thought of even before *doing* good?'

The question was very simple; but I knew well that eye and voice would compel an answer, however unwilling. Edward possesses, in a rare degree, the power of making people find out what they mean, or whether they mean anything—a valuable gift, where meanings, or no meanings, are apt to shelter themselves under a veil of vague sentences.

'What?' asked Kate, lifting her grey eyes to his face, with grave, thoughtful wonder.

'*Being* good; being must come before doing.'

Her glance fell. 'And if one is not good, Mr Grey?'

'In the true sense we are none of us that; but there

are certain lessons we must learn before we can teach them to others. The Bible direction is, "Let him that heareth say, Come," which implies that we have first come ourselves. It is not "*Go,*" but "*Come*—come and drink with me; *I* am standing by the fountain, fresh and full and free; *my* thirst is quenched."'

'Ah! no—no,' she broke in impetuously; 'I don't understand that, Mr Grey, and so I suppose this must be the reason I can't get on with my class, or my district, because I only say "Go," and not "Come."'

A look answered her, and she was uneasily silent for some minutes, tracing diagrams on the sand with the point of her parasol.

'What must I do?' she asked, at length.

'Come yourself to the Saviour. It's no use going out to water the ground unless you are drawing from the living well. You may do more harm than good; for if you are not a channel between the two, you may be a barrier.'

'But, Mr Grey,' pleaded Kate, 'I do ask God's help for my work.'

'I do not doubt that; but forgive me this once if I speak plainly: do you ask it for yourself? Have you come to feel your need of help and mercy as a sinner in God's sight; and are you seeking the new birth from above, without which—they are Christ's words, not mine —you cannot enter His kingdom? Have you, like the disciples of old, left all and followed Him?'

'Left all!' said Kate, while a troubled flush mounted to cheek and brow; 'It's not easy!'

'Ah! you have not got the motive power. Love sees no difficulties, grudges no sacrifice. But where love is wanting, there must always be the heavy yoke and the hard service.'

'But I can't *make* myself love,' she replied, a little impatiently.

'No; but you can *pray* to love—to have Christ so revealed to you that you must love Him—to have His love shed abroad in your heart by the Holy Spirit. And the promise is sure, "Ask"—only ask—"and ye shall receive."'

They were plain truths, but she needed them. And I believe that, by God's great mercy, they penetrated into her heart, slowly indeed, but surely, bringing new thoughts, aims, and prayers, which were in time to over-turn the dream-world in which she had been living. I did not hear her answer, for the sand-castle was finished, and I drew the little builders away.

'What bits of freshness children are!' said Helen, joining me a few moments afterwards, as I sat watching their play; 'their delight never flags for a moment, while our very pleasure-taking has a kind of serious business about it. And then it is sometimes so difficult not to feel as if one had come to the end of everything.'

'Isn't that a morbid mood?' I ventured to suggest.

'Undoubtedly; but you see, my dear wise Elsie, you,

with your full, busy life, so rich in love and duty, can scarcely understand how hard it is *not* to be morbid. Besides, listen to that ringing laugh! Who ever grew morbid within sound of such music ?'

These last words were spoken with a tremulous quiver, and the mournful eyes that looked out upon the sea, were shining through tears. Even the strongest are weak sometimes, but the tokens of their weakness are rare and few. I hardly knew how to answer her; but it is such a comfort for those who are not gifted with ready speech, that we have always better words at command than any of our own. I went back to my own old resting-place in years gone by, and whispered softly—

'He shall choose our heritage for us.'

'Ah! yes,' she answered. ' "Who knoweth what is good for man in this life ?"

"*I* might have chosen a love-lit hearth, instead of love and heaven ;
   A single rose for a rose-tree, that beareth seven times seven."'

'And by and by we shall know the reason of all these things.'

'By and by. But after all, Elsie, I never find much help in that. We are not angels—we are living *now*, and not by and by. The rest "remains" with God, but the suffering is present; and sometimes,' she added, speaking low and a little bitterly, 'the doubt and the darkness are present too.'

'So that, after all, we come back to the old prayer, "Lord, increase our faith; help us to trust thy word that all is well, and to leave the understanding of it till we get home." Don't you think we might be lifted out of darkness into abiding light, if we would only throw ourselves simply, entirely, helplessly, upon the strong, unseen Hand, which can raise us to "heavenly places," even here? "The power of the Holy Ghost"—how little we know about that, Helen, how little we prove it! And yet it is through this that we are to "abound in hope," though it *is* "here" and "now" with us, and the better country is out of sight.'

But already the children were back, and there was no time for further talk. Yet I knew now, if I had doubted before, that Helen had not *fought* her battle, but was fighting it all the while, often with sinking heart and wearied hand. Thus, perhaps, she was fitted for her work: for they whose own wounds are scarcely closed, can best soothe the wounds of others: and they who struggle in deadly strife with the tempter can best succour the tempted. For they know that, as the smart is real, so the healing is real too. The 'other Comforter' is near them, not a dream or an idea, but living, and loving, and true. They have heard His voice, and felt His touch in their own agony, and they go forth from His presence to 'speak of what they do know, and testify that they have seen.' In the slow silent hours, measured out by throbs of pain, in the terrible conflict, which only God and His angels watch, are learned the faith which strengthens a weaker brother, and the wise, loving sympathy which falls upon the mourner's heart like dew on drooping flowers.

Still we lingered, breathing in the salt freshness of the sea, long after children and nurses had been sent home—long after the moonlight had begun to fall with a silver sheen upon sand and water, and weed-covered rocks, and upon the little fishing-boats which glided out of the harbour with their sails all set, as if they might be passing silently to some unknown shore.

'How long are you going to stay, Elsie—till midnight?' asked my husband, coming up to Helen and me as we stood a little apart, not speaking, but watching the soft light upon sea and land, and the 'glory of the stars,' as they looked out one by one from the purple sky.

'Hush!' said Helen, catching her breath suddenly to listen, for we heard a succession of dull heavy thumps, mingling at intervals with the roar of the tide. 'Ah! it must be the band at Deerfoot. I hear a faint echo of music now, a sort of thrill upon the air, and the drum is distinct enough: but how meaningless it sounds without the instruments!'

'Is not that a sort of parable, Miss Hamilton? There are harmonies of which we only catch the echoes now and then—echoes without meaning, as they seem to us, nay, often full of discord. But that is only because we hear a part, and not the whole. If we will only have patience.'

'Yes,' said Helen, her eyes flashing with a sudden light; 'the broken echoes will be linked together by and by, and the grand, full harmony will be complete, and we shall know then that even the discords had their place. Not now,' she added softly, 'not now; but it is only a little while to wait.'

.   .   .   .

And did Miss Hamilton marry Captain Raeburn? I am quite aware that she ought to have done, to make my story complete; but, in point of fact, she did not. I sometimes think, however, that he will take Kate back with him to India.

Then did Miss Hamilton become a deaconess? Not in name, certainly, but as certainly in fact. I am often struck by the contrast between Helen and Mary Wilton. In one thing they are alike, they have each lost their dearest, Mary more entirely even than Helen. The sea shall give up its dead, but from the grave of a buried trust there is no resurrection. And they are both solitary—both living rather for all who need them, than for one only, and yet each fills a different niche, and is doing a different work.

Helen, with her health and energy, is like Phœbe of old, 'a servant of the Church,' going in the strength of her womanly tenderness—nay, in a higher than this, in that of faith and prayer—to carry to dark homes a ray of everlasting light, or stretching out the gentle hand which, in its purity, shrinks not from the touch of pollution, to rescue some outcast sister from the downward path. It is curious what power she seems to have even over the wildest and most unruly spirits. I have seen our rough sailors, whom my husband has in vain endeavoured to influence, cease their brawls when they saw 'the lady' approach, and listen to her, half in reverence, half in wonder, with the docile attention of children. And I have seen young women, bold and hardened, fast losing all their womanliness, yield to her persuasive teaching, and suffer her to lead them back to themselves and to their God.

Mary, on the contrary, 'dwells among her own people,' clothed in the grace of meek, unselfish endurance, and full of sweet, harmonious thoughts and words. She lives so constantly in the realized presence of Christ, that her very look is a quiet sermon, which seems to bring Him near. And she is busy too, in her way; claimed in turn by each member of a large circle, and filling, as 'Aunt Mary,' a place hardly less important than if she had added to her name the dignified prefix of Mrs.

They are types of distinct classes, these two, each needing the other as the complement of itself. There is room for both in the Master's vineyard : let them lay aside all jealousy and depreciation one of another, and accept their separate service as His appointment.

And we, to whom God has given the love of husband and child, could not well do without these 'unattached.' For though we are apt to smile at old maids' theories, we can sometimes see our duties better by the light thereof, and certainly we are often glad of their help in divers emergencies. And there are fields of usefulness which they can cultivate better than we, though it may be that the work done there meets with little appreciation except from Him who 'seeth in secret.'

But now I must really conclude, for I am beginning to wander into prosy disquisitions which no one will care to read. And, after all, my story is so very simple and ordinary, that I rather fear it has been a waste of time to record it. However, I have often wished that some woman like myself would write the story of her everyday life, with its mistakes and failures, and tell me what had corrected the one and encouraged her in the other. And this is just what I have myself attempted.

Looking back over it all, from the particular point where I now stand, the summer past, and the autumn well on its way, I cannot feel, as I fancy many could— Grace, for instance, or Helen Hamilton,—that I have accomplished any definite work. But perhaps it is not given to all to feel this; and it may be that some lives will always appear incomplete, because we cannot see the whole of which they form a part. The stones which are lying about under the workman's hand seem to have no purpose or meaning; but when they are fitted to their place in the building, we shall be able to discover both. That which shall be appears not now; but faith comes in where sight fails, and so I must believe that God is shaping my life to His own ends, though I cannot know them yet.

Perhaps they may grow more clear to me by and by, if I am spared much longer, when the desert life is almost done, and I pitch my tent by the river brink, and sit down in the light of the sinking to think it all over before I pass to the other side. But, at any rate, I know that once there, all will be made plain.

And one thing I can say, even now—oh, how thankfully, how joyfully!

'Hitherto hath the Lord helped me.'

THE END.

Crawford & M'Cabe, Printers, 15 Queen Street, Edinburgh

LIST OF WORKS

PUBLISHED BY

JOHNSTONE, HUNTER, & CO., EDINBURGH.

MAGAZINES:—

The Christian Treasury; Containing Contributions from Ministers and Members of various Evangelical Denominations. Edited by HORATIUS BONAR, D.D. Super royal 8vo.

Monthly Parts,	-	-	-	-	£0 0 6
Weekly Numbers,	-	-	-	-	0 0 1

The Children's Hour; A Monthly Magazine for our Young Folks. Edited by M. H., Author of "Rosa Lindesay," etc. Crown 8vo. Beautifully Illustrated, - - - - 0 0 3

The Reformed Presbyterian Magazine; Containing Home and Missionary Intelligence relating to the Reformed Presbyterian Church in Scotland. Demy 8vo. Monthly, - - 0 0 4

J. H. & CO.'S SIXPENNY SERIES.

Super royal 32mo, cloth limp. Illustrated.

1. JEANIE HAY, THE CHEERFUL GIVER. And other Tales.
2. LILY RAMSAY; OR, HANDSOME IS WHO HANDSOME DOES. And other Tales.
3. ARCHIE DOUGLAS; OR, WHERE THERE'S A WILL THERE'S A WAY. And other Tales.
4. MINNIE AND LETTY; OR, THE EXPECTED ARRIVAL. And other Tales.
5. NED FAIRLIE AND HIS RICH UNCLE. And other Tales.
6. MR GRANVILLE'S JOURNEY. And other Tales.
7. JAMIE WILSON'S ADVENTURES. And other Tales.
8. THE TWO FRIENDS. And other Tales.
9. THE TURNIP LANTERN. And other Tales.
10. JOHN BUTLER; OR, THE BLIND MAN'S DOG. And other Tales.
11. CHRISTFRIED'S FIRST JOURNEY. And other Tales.
12. KATIE WATSON, THE CONTENTED LACEMAKER. And other Tales.
13. BIDDY, THE MAID OF ALL WORK.
14. MAGGIE MORRIS: A TALE OF THE DEVONSHIRE MOOR.

J. H. & CO.'S SHILLING PACKETS OF REWARD BOOKS.

Super Royal 32mo, in Illuminated Covers.

1. SHORT TALES TO EXPLAIN HOMELY PROVERBS. By M. H. A Series of Twelve Penny Books. Illustrated.
2. SHORT STORIES TO EXPLAIN BIBLE TEXTS. By M. H. A Series of Twelve Penny Books. Illustrated.

J. H. & CO.'S SHILLING PACKETS OF REWARD BOOKS—*Continued.*

    3. WISE SAYINGS, AND STORIES TO EXPLAIN THEM. By M. H. A Series of Twelve Penny Books. Illustrated.

    4. LITTLE TALES FOR LITTLE PEOPLE. A Series of Six Twopenny Books. Illustrated.

J. H. & CO.'S ONE SHILLING SERIES.

    Super royal 32mo, extra cloth, bevelled boards, Illustrated.

    1. THE STORY OF A RED VELVET BIBLE. By M. H.

    2. ALICE LOWTHER ; OR, GRANDMAMMA'S STORY ABOUT HER LITTLE RED BIBLE. By J. W. C.

    3. NOTHING TO DO ; OR, THE INFLUENCE OF A LIFE. By M. H.

    4. ALFRED AND THE LITTLE DOVE. By the Rev. F. A. Krummacher, D.D. And THE YOUNG SAVOYARD. By Ernest Hold.

    5. MARY M'NEILL ; OR, THE WORD REMEMBERED. A Tale of Humble Life. By J. W. C.

    6. HENRY MORGAN ; OR, THE SOWER AND THE SEED. By M. H.

    7. WITLESS WILLIE, THE IDIOT BOY. By the Author of "Mary Matheson," etc.

    8. MARY MANSFIELD ; OR, NO TIME TO BE A CHRISTIAN. By M. H.

    9. FRANK FIELDING ; OR, DEBTS AND DIFFICULTIES. By Agnes Veitch.

    10. TALES FOR "THE CHILDREN'S HOUR." By M. M. C.

    11. THE LITTLE CAPTAIN : a Tale of the Sea. By Mrs George Cupples.

    12. GOTTFRIED OF THE IRON HAND : a Tale of German Chivalry.

    13. ARTHUR FORTESCUE ; OR, THE SCHOOLBOY HERO. By Robert Hope Moncrieff.

    14. THE SANGREAL ; OR, THE HIDDEN TREASURE. By M. H.

    15. COCKERILL THE CONJURER ; OR, THE BRAVE BOY OF HAMELN.

    16. JOTTINGS FROM THE DIARY OF THE SUN. By M. H.

    17. DOWN AMONG THE WATER WEEDS. By Mona B. Bickerstaffe.

J. H. & CO.'S EIGHTEENPENCE SERIES.

    Super royal 32mo, extra cloth, richly gilt sides and edges, Illustrated.

    1. SHORT TALES TO EXPLAIN HOMELY PROVERBS. By M. H.

    2. SHORT STORIES TO EXPLAIN BIBLE TEXTS. By M. H.

    3. ALFRED AND THE LITTLE DOVE. By the Rev. F. A. Krummacher, D.D. And WITLESS WILLIE, THE IDIOT BOY. By the Author of "Mary Matheson," etc.

    4. THE STORY OF A RED VELVET BIBLE : and HENRY MORGAN ; OR, THE SOWER AND THE SEED. By M. H., Editor of "The Children's Hour."

    5. ARTHUR FORTESCUE ; OR, THE SCHOOLBOY HERO. By Robert Hope Moncrieff. And FRANK FIELDING ; OR, DEBTS AND DIFFICULTIES. By Agnes Veitch.

    6. MARY M'NEILL ; OR, THE WORD REMEMBERED. By J. W. C. And other Tales.

    7. ALICE LOWTHER ; OR, GRANDMAMMA'S STORY ABOUT HER LITTLE RED BIBLE. By J. W. C. And other Tales.

    8. NOTHING TO DO; OR, THE INFLUENCE OF A LIFE : and MARY MANSFIELD ; OR, NO TIME TO BE A CHRISTIAN. By M. H.

    9. BILL MARLIN'S TALES OF THE SEA. By Mrs George Cupples.

    10. GOTTFRIED OF THE IRON HAND. And other Tales.

    11. THE STORY OF THE KIRK : a Sketch of Scottish Church History. By Robert Naismith.

    12. THE HIDDEN TREASURE. And other Tales. By M. H.

    13. LITTLE TALES FOR LITTLE PEOPLE. By Various Authors.

    14. WISE SAYINGS, AND STORIES TO EXPLAIN THEM. By M. H.

J. H. & CO.'S HALF-CROWN SERIES.

Extra fcap. 8vo, handsomely bound in cloth.

1. ROSA LINDSAY, THE LIGHT OF KILMAIN. By M. H. Illustrated.
2. NEWLYN HOUSE, THE HOME OF THE DAVENPORTS. By A. E. W. Illustrated.
3. ALICE THORNE; OR, A SISTER'S WORK. Illustrated.
4. LABOURERS IN THE VINEYARD. By M. H. Illustrated.
5. THE CHILDREN OF THE GREAT KING. By M. H. Illustrated.
6. LITTLE HARRY'S TROUBLES. By the Author of "Gottfried." Illustrated.
7. SUNDAY SCHOOL PHOTOGRAPHS. By the Rev. Alfred Taylor, Bristol, Pennsylvania.
8. WAYMARKS FOR THE GUIDING OF LITTLE FEET. By the Rev. J. A. Wallace.
9. THE DOMESTIC CIRCLE; OR, THE RELATIONS, RESPONSIBILITIES, AND DUTIES OF HOME LIFE. By the Rev. John Thomson. Illustrated.
10. SELECT CHRISTIAN BIOGRAPHIES. By the Rev. James Gardner, A.M., M.D. Illustrated.
11. OCEAN LAYS. Selected by the Rev. J. Longmuir, LL.D. Illustrated.
12. WILBERFORCE'S PRACTICAL VIEW OF CHRISTIANITY. Complete Edition.
13. COMMUNION SERVICES, ACCORDING TO THE PRESBYTERIAN FORM. By the Rev. J. A. Wallace.
14. ATTITUDES AND ASPECTS OF THE DIVINE REDEEMER. By Rev. J. A. Wallace.
15. THE REDEEMER AND THE REDEMPTION. By the Rev. Alex. S. Patterson, D.D.
16. A PASTOR'S LEGACY. Edited by the Rev. J. A. Wallace.
17. JAMES NISBET; A STUDY FOR YOUNG MEN. By the Rev. J. A. Wallace.
18. NOBLE RIVERS, AND STORIES CONCERNING THEM. By Anna J. Buckland. Illustrated.

J. H. & CO.'S THREE SHILLING SERIES.

Extra fcap. 8vo, richly gilt sides and edges.

1. MISS MATTY; OR, OUR YOUNGEST PASSENGER. And other Tales. Illustrated.
2. HORACE HAZELWOOD; OR, LITTLE THINGS. And other Tales. Illustrated.
3. ROSA LINDSAY, THE LIGHT OF KILMAIN. By M. H. Illustrated.
4. NEWLYN HOUSE, THE HOME OF THE DAVENPORTS. By A. E. W. Illustrated.
5. ALICE THORNE; OR, A SISTER'S WORK. Illustrated.
6. LABOURERS IN THE VINEYARD. By M. H. Illustrated.
7. LITTLE HARRY'S TROUBLES. By the Author of "Gottfried." Illustrated.
8. THE CHILDREN OF THE GREAT KING. By M. H. Illustrated.
9. THE DOMESTIC CIRCLE; OR, THE RELATIONS, RESPONSIBILITIES, AND DUTIES OF HOME LIFE. By the Rev. John Thomson. Illustrated.
10. SUNDAY SCHOOL PHOTOGRAPHS. By the Rev. Alfred Taylor, Bristol.
11. WAYMARKS FOR THE GUIDING OF LITTLE FEET. By the Rev. J. A. Wallace.
12. SELECT CHRISTIAN BIOGRAPHIES. By the Rev. James Gardner, A.M., M.D. Illustrated.
13. CARDIPHONIA; OR, THE UTTERANCE OF THE HEART. In a Series of Letters. By John Newton. A New Edition, bevelled boards, cut edges.
14. FOUND AFLOAT. By Mrs George Cupples. And other Tales. Illustrated.
15. JAMES NISBET; A STUDY FOR YOUNG MEN. By the Rev. J. A. Wallace.
16. THE WHITE ROE OF GLENMERE. By Mona B. Bickerstaffe. And other Tales. Illustrated.
17. NOBLE RIVERS, AND STORIES CONCERNING THEM. By Anna J. Buckland. Illustrated.

J. H. & CO.'S FIVE SHILLING SERIES.

Bound in cloth, bevelled boards, richly gilt sides and edges.

1. THE CHILDREN'S HOUR ANNUAL. First Series. 656 pp. Extra fcap. 8vo. Illustrated.
2. THE CHILDREN'S HOUR ANNUAL. Second Series. 640 pp. Extra fcap. 8vo. Illustrated.
3. SKETCHES OF SCRIPTURE CHARACTERS. By the Rev. Andrew Thomson, D.D. Crown 8vo. Illustrated.
4. STARS OF EARTH; OR, WILD FLOWERS OF THE MONTHS. By Leigh Page. Crown 8vo. With Original Illustrations by the Author.
5. ELIJAH; THE DESERT PROPHET: A Biography. By the Rev. H. T. Howat. Crown 8vo. Illustrated.

Afflicted's Refuge (The); or, Prayers adapted to various Circum-
stances of Distress. Fcap. 8vo, cloth,   -   -   -   £0 2 6

Alfred and the Little Dove. By F. A. Krummacher, D.D. And the
Young Savoyard. By Ernest Hold. Translated from the German
by a Lady. Royal 32mo, cloth, Illustrated, -   -   -   0 1 0

Alice Lowther; or, Grandmamma's Story about her Little Red
Bible. By J. W. C., Author of "Mary M'Neill," etc. Royal 32mo,
cloth, Illustrated.   -   -   -   -   -   -   0 1 0

Alice Thorne; or, A Sister's Work.
Extra fcap. 8vo, cloth, Illustrated, -   -   -   -   0 2 6

———— Extra cloth, gilt edges,   -   -   -   -   0 3 0

Archie Douglas; or, Where there's a Will there's a Way. And
other Tales. Super Royal 32mo, cloth, Illustrated, -   -   0 0 6

Arthur Fortescue; or, The Schoolboy Hero.
By Robert Hope Moncrieff. Royal 32mo, cloth, Illustrated,   -   0 1 0

Authorised Standards of the Free Church of Scotland:
Being the Westminster Confession of Faith and other Documents.
Published by Authority of the General Assembly. Demy 12mo, cloth
limp,   -   -   -   -   -   -   -   -   0 1 3

———— Cloth boards,   -   -   -   -   -   0 1 6

———— Superior Edition, Printed on Superfine Paper, extra cloth, bevelled
boards, antique, -   -   -   -   -   -   0 2 6

———— Full calf, lettered, antique, -   -   -   -   0 5 0

Biddy, the Maid of All Work.
Super Royal 32mo, cloth, Illustrated,   -   -   -   0 0 6

Bill Marlin's Tales of the Sea.
By Mrs George Cupples. Super royal 32mo, extra cloth, gilt edges,
Illustrated,   -   -   -   -   -   -   -   0 1 6

Brodie (Rev. James, A.M.) The Antiquity and Nature of Man:
A Reply to Sir Charles Lyell's Recent Work. Extra fcap. 8vo, cloth,   0 2 6

———— Papers Offered for Discussion at the Meeting of the British
Association at Dundee. Extra fcap. 8vo, boards,   -   -   0 1 0

———— The Rational Creation: An Inquiry into the Nature and
Classification of Rational Creatures, and the Government which God
exercises over them. Crown 8vo, cloth,   -   -   -   0 5 0

———— An Inquiry into the Apocalypse, with an Endeavour to ascertain our present Position on the Chart of Time. Royal 8vo, sewed,   0 2 0

Brodie (Rev. James, A. M.) Memoir of Annie M'Donald Christie,
a Self-taught Cottager. Demy 18mo, cloth, - - - £0 1 6

Buckland (Anna J.) Noble Rivers, and Stories concerning Them.
Extra fcap. 8vo, cloth, with Illustrations, - - - 0 2 6
———— Extra cloth, gilt edges, - - - - 0 3 0

Burns (Rev. George, D.D.) Prayers for the Use of Sabbath Schools.
18mo, sewed, - - - - - - 0 0 4

Catechisms—

THE ASSEMBLY'S SHORTER CATECHISM ; with References to the
Scripture Proofs. Demy 18mo, stitched, - - - 0 0 0½

THE ASSEMBLY'S SHORTER CATECHISM ; with (*Italicised*) Proofs from
Scripture at full length ; also with Additional Scripture References,
selected from Boston, Fisher, M. Henry, Paterson, Vincent, and
others. Demy 18mo, stitched, - - - - 0 0 1

THE ASSEMBLY'S LARGER CATECHISM ; with (*Italicised*) Proofs from
Scripture at full length. Demy 12mo, sewed, - - 0 0 6

CATECHISM OF THE EVIDENCES OF REVEALED RELIGION, with a few
Preliminary Questions on Natural Religion. By William Ferrie,
D.D., Kilconquhar. 18mo, stitched, - - - 0 0 4

CATECHISM ON BAPTISM : in which are considered its Nature, its
Subjects, and the Obligations resulting from it. By the late
Henry Grey, D.D., Edinburgh. 18mo, stitched, - - 0 0 6

THE CHILD'S FIRST CATECHISM. 48mo, stitched, - - 0 0 0½

SHORT CATECHISM FOR YOUNG CHILDREN. By the Rev. John Brown,
Haddington. 32mo, stitched, - - - - 0 0 0½

PLAIN CATECHISM FOR CHILDREN. By the Rev. Matthew Henry.
18mo, stitched, - - - - - - 0 0 1

FIFTY QUESTIONS CONCERNING THE LEADING DOCTRINES AND DUTIES
OF THE GOSPEL ; with Scripture Answers and Parallel Texts. For
the use of Sabbath Schools. 18mo, stitched, - - 0 0 1

FORM OF EXAMINATION BEFORE THE COMMUNION. Approved by the
General Assembly of the Kirk of Scotland (1592), and appointed
to be read in Families and Schools ; with Proofs from Scripture
(commonly known as "Craig's Catechism"). With a Recommendatory Note by the Rev. Dr Candlish, Rev. Alexander Moody
Stuart, and Rev. Dr Horatius Bonar. 18mo, stitched, - 0 0 1

THE MOTHER'S CATECHISM ; being a Preparatory Help for the Young
and Ignorant, to their easier understanding The Assembly's
Shorter Catechism. By the Rev. John Willison, Dundee. 32mo,
stitched, - - - - - - - 0 0 1

WATTS' (DR ISAAC) JUVENILE HISTORICAL CATECHISMS OF THE OLD
AND NEW TESTAMENTS ; with Numerous Scripture References, and
a Selection of Hymns. Demy 18mo, stitched, - - 0 0 1

A SCRIPTURE CATECHISM, Historical and Doctrinal, for the use of
Schools and Families. By John Whitecross, Author of "Anec-
dotes on the Shorter Catechism," etc. 18mo, stitched, - 0 0 1

A SUMMARY OF CHRISTIAN DOCTRINE AND DUTIES ; being the Westminster Assembly's Shorter Catechism, without the Questions,
with Marginal References. Fcap. 8vo, stitched, - - 0 0 1

Children of the Great King (The): A Story of the Crimean War.
By M. H., Editor of "The Children's Hour." Extra fcap. 8vo,
cloth, with Illustrations, - - - - 0 2 6
———— Cloth extra, gilt edges, - - - - 0 3 0

Children's Hour (The) Annual. First Series.
656 pp., and upwards of 50 Illustrations. Extra fcap. 8vo, cloth, gilt edges, - - - - - - - £0 5 0

—— **Second Series.**
640 pp., and upwards of 70 Illustrations. Extra fcap. 8vo, cloth, gilt edges, - - - - - - 0 5 0

Children's Hour (The) Series of Gift Books.
1. MISS MATTY; OR, OUR YOUNGEST PASSENGER. And other Tales.
2. HORACE HAZELWOOD. And other Tales.
3. FOUND AFLOAT. And other Tales.
4. THE WHITE ROE OF GLENMERE. And other Tales.
     Extra fcap. 8vo, cloth, gilt sides and edges, Illustrated—each   0 3 0

Christfried's First Journey. And other Tales.
Super royal 32mo, cloth, Illustrated, - - - 0 0 6

Christian Treasury (The) Volumes 1845 to 1860.
16 Volumes, royal 8vo, cloth—each - - - 0 5 0
     A complete Set will be forwarded to any part of the country, carriage paid, on receipt of £3, 3s.

—— **Volumes 1861, 1862, 1863, 1864, 1865, and 1866.**
Super royal 8vo, cloth, green and gold—each - - 0 6 6

Cockerill the Conjurer; or, The Brave Boy of Hameln. By the
Author of "Little Harry's Troubles." Super royal 32mo, cloth, bevelled boards, Illustrated, - - - - 0 1 0

Confession of Faith (The) agreed upon at the Assembly of
Divines at Westminster. Complete Edition, with the *Italics* of the elegant Quarto Edition of 1658 restored. (Authorised Edition.)
Demy 12mo, cloth limp, - - - - 0 1 0
——— Cloth boards, - - - - - 0 1 3
——— Superior Edition, Printed on Superfine Paper, extra cloth, bevelled boards, antique, - - - - - 0 2 6
——— Full calf, lettered, antique, - - - 0 5 0

Dill (Edward Marcus, A.M., M.D.) The Mystery Solved: or,
Ireland's Miseries: Their Grand Cause and Cure. Fcap. 8vo, cloth, 0 2 6

—— **The Gathering Storm; or, Britain's Romeward Career: A**
Warning and Appeal to British Protestants. Fcap. 8vo, cloth, 0 1 0

Down among the Water Weeds; or Marvels of Pond Life.
By Mona B. Bickerstaffe. Super royal 32mo, cloth, bevelled boards, with numerous Illustrations, - - - - 0 1 0

Family Prayers for Working Men.
By Ministers of Various Evangelical Denominations. Edited with a Preface by the Rev. John Hall, D.D., Dublin. Extra fcap. 8vo—
Common Edition, stiffened boards, - - - 0 0 6
——— limp cloth, - - - - 0 0 9
Fine Edition, bevelled boards, - - - 0 1 6

Forbes (Rev. Robert, A.M.) Procedure in the Inferior Courts of
the Free Church of Scotland. With Appendix, embracing a Ministerial Manual; with Forms and Documents.
         (Third Edition in Preparation.)

Found Afloat. By Mrs George Cupples. And other Tales.
Extra fcap. 8vo, with Illustrations. Cloth, gilt edges, - 0 3 0

Frank Fielding ; or, Debts and Difficulties.
A Story for Boys. By Agnes Veitch, Author of "Woodruffe," etc.
Royal 32mo, bevelled boards, - - - - £0 1 0

Gardner (Rev. James, A.M., M.D.) Select Christian Biographies.
Extra fcap. 8vo, cloth, with Illustrations, - - - 0 2 6

———— Cloth extra, gilt edges, - - - 0 3 6

Gottfried of the Iron Hand : A Tale of German Chivalry.
By the Author of "Little Harry's Troubles." Royal 32mo, cloth,
Illustrated, - - - - - 0 1 0

Habit; with Special Reference to the Formation of a Virtuous
Character. An Address to Students. By Burns Thomson. With
a Recommendatory Note by the late Professor Miller. 18mo,
Second Edition, revised, - - - - 0 0 2

Henry Morgan; or, The Sower and the Seed.
By M. H., Editor of "The Children's Hour." Royal 32mo, cloth,
Illustrated, - - - - - - 0 1 0

Hidden Treasure (The). And other Tales.
By M. H., Editor of "The Children's Hour." Super royal 32mo,
cloth extra, gilt edges, Illustrated, - - - 0 1 6

Horace Hazelwood; or, Little Things.
By Robert Hope Moncrieff. And other Tales. Extra fcap. 8vo,
with Illustrations, cloth, gilt edges, - - - 0 3 0

Howat (Rev. H. T.) Elijah; the Desert Prophet. A Biography.
Crown 8vo, cloth, gilt edges, with Illustrations, - - 0 5 0

———— Sabbath Hours : A Series of Meditations on Gospel Themes.
Extra fcap. 8vo, cloth, - - - - 0 3 6

Hunter (James J.) Historical Notices of Lady Yester's Church
and Parish, Edinburgh. Compiled from Authentic Sources. Extra
fcap. 8vo, cloth, Printed on Toned Paper, - - 0 2 6

Hymns for the Use of Sabbath Schools and Bible Classes.
Selected by a Committee of Clergymen. Royal 32mo, sewed, - 0 0 3

Jamie Wilson's Adventures. And other Tales.
Super royal 32mo, cloth, Illustrated, - - - 0 0 6

Jeanie Hay, the Cheerful Giver. And other Tales.
Super royal 32mo, cloth, Illustrated, - - - 0 0 6

John Butler; or, The Blind Man's Dog. And other Tales.
Super royal 32mo, cloth, Illustrated, - - - 0 0 6

Jottings from the Diary of the Sun.
By M. H., Editor of "The Children's Hour." Super royal 32mo,
cloth, bevelled boards, Illustrated, - - - 0 1 0

Katie Watson. And other Tales.
Super royal 32mo, cloth, Illustrated, - - - 0 0 6

Labourers in the Vineyard; or, Dioramic Scenes from the Lives
of Eminent Christians. With Recommendatory Preface, by the
Rev. A. K. H. Boyd, D.D., St Andrews. Extra fcap. 8vo, cloth,
with Illustrations, - - - - - 0 2 6

———————— Cloth extra, gilt edges, - - - 0 3 0

Lily Ramsay; or, Handsome Is who Handsome Does. And other
Tales. Super royal 32mo, cloth, Illustrated, -   -   -   £0 0 6

Little Captain (The): A Tale of the Sea,
By Mrs George Cupples. Royal 32mo, cloth, Illustrated,   -   0 1 0

Little Harry's Troubles: A Story of Gipsy Life.
By the Author of " Gottfried of the Iron Hand." Extra fcap. 8vo,
cloth, with Illustrations,   -   -   -   -   -   0 2 6
———— Cloth extra, gilt edges,   -   -   -   -   0 3 0

Little Tales for Little People. A Series of Twopenny Reward
Books. By Various Authors.   With Illustrations.

    1. John Butler; or, The Blind Man's Dog.
       Rosedale Villa; or, The Grey Parrot.
    2. Asta Von Flotow; or, "The Cuckoo's Warning."
       The Two Blackbirds; or, Jealousy.
    3. Charles Harley; or, The Bag of Marbles.
       Stanley Hollins; or, The Spider and the Silkworms.
    4. Christfried's First Journey.
    5. Katie Watson, the Contented Lacemaker.
       The Twin Brothers: A Ragged School Reminiscence.
    6. Willie Smith: A Scottish Story.
       Alice and Fanny; or, Disobedience Punished.

    Done up in a neat Illuminated Packet. Super royal 32mo,   0 1 0
    In cloth extra, gilt edges,   -   -   -   -   0 1 6

M'Donald (Rev. John, Calcutta). The Suffering Saviour.
With a Preface, by the late Rev. W. K. Tweedie, D.D.   Royal 32mo,
limp cloth,   -   -   -   -   -   -   0 0 6

Maggie Morris: A Tale of the Devonshire Moor.
Super royal 32mo, cloth, Illustrated,   -   -   -   0 0 6

Mary M'Neill; or, The Word Remembered.
A Tale of Humble Life. By J. W. C., Author of " Alice Lowther,"
etc. Royal 32mo, cloth, Illustrated,   -   -   -   0 1 0

Mary Mansfield; or, No Time to be a Christian.
By M. H., Editor of " The Children's Hour." Royal 32mo, cloth,
Illustrated,   -   -   -   -   -   -   0 1 0

Meikle (Rev. James, D.D.) Coming Events.
An Inquiry regarding the Three Prophetical Numbers of the last
Chapter of Daniel. Extra fcap. 8vo, cloth,   -   -   -   0 2 6

———— **The Battle of Armageddon; and its Results.**
An Exposition of the Sixth and Seventh Vials of the Apocalypse.
And also an Inquiry regarding the Commencement of the 1260
Symbolical Days. Crown 8vo, cloth,   -   -   -   0 3 6

———— **The Edenic Dispensation.**
Fcap. 8vo, cloth,   -   -   -   -   -   0 3 6

———— **The Nature of the Mediatorial Dispensation.**
Crown 8vo, cloth,   -   -   -   -   -   0 3 6

———— **The Administration of the Mediatorial Dispensation.**
Crown 8vo, cloth,   -   -   -   -   -   0 3 6

Miller (Rev. James N.) Prelacy Tried by the Word of God.
With an Appendix on the Prelatic Argument from Church History.
Fcap. 8vo, limp cloth, - - - - £0 1 0

Miller (Professor James). Physiology in Harmony with the Bible,
respecting the Value and Right Observance of the Sabbath. Royal
32mo, limp cloth, - - - 0 0 6

Minnie and Letty; or, the Expected Arrival. And other Tales.
Super royal 32mo, cloth, Illustrated, - - - 0 0 6

Miss Matty; or, Our Youngest Passenger.
By Mrs George Cupples. And other Tales. Extra fcap. 8vo, with
Illustrations, cloth, gilt edges, - - - 0 3 0

Mr Granville's Journey. And other Tales.
Super royal 32mo, cloth, Illustrated, - - - 0 0 6

MUSIC—

The Treasury Hymnal, a Selection of Part Music, in the
ordinary Notation, with Instrumental Accompaniment; the
Hymns selected from Dr Bonar's "Hymns of Faith and Hope."
The Letter Note Method of Musical Notation, by permission of
Messrs Colville and Bentley, is added as a help to young singers.

No. 1.	FORWARD, - - -	Old Melody.
	A BETHLEHEM HYMN,	Arranged from Mozart.
2.	THE FRIEND, -	Haydn.
	LOST BUT FOUND, -	Pleyel.
3.	A LITTLE WHILE, -	Adapted from Mendelssohn.
	A STRANGER HERE, -	Pleyel.
4.	THE BLANK, - -	Pleyel.
	THE NIGHT AND THE MORNING,	Adapted from Rode.
5.	THE CLOUDLESS, -	Haydn.
	THE SUBSTITUTE, -	Haydn.
6.	THY WAY, NOT MINE, -	Altered from Pleyel.
	REST YONDER, -	Steibelt.
7.	EVER NEAR, -	German Melody.
	QUIS SEPARABIT, -	Beethoven.
8.	ALL WELL, -	Haydn.
	DISAPPOINTMENT, -	Haydn.
	CHILD'S PRAYER, -	Weber.
9.	GOD'S ISRAEL, -	Atterbury.
	THE ELDER BROTHER,	Beethoven.
	DAY SPRING, -	German Melody.
10.	THE NIGHT COMETH, -	Venetian Melody.
	HOW LONG, - -	Mendelssohn.
11.	THE TWO ERAS, -	Spohr.
	THE SHEPHERD'S PLAIN,	Whitaker.
12.	BRIGHT FEET OF MAY,	Whitaker.
	HEAVEN AT LAST, -	Clementi.

The above in stiffened wrapper. Super royal 8vo, - 0 1 0
Single Nos.—each - - - - 0 0 1

A Graduated Course of Elementary Instruction in Singing
ON THE LETTER NOTE METHOD (*by means of which any difficulty
of learning to Sing from the common Notation can be easily over-
come*) in 26 Lessons. By David Colville and George Bentley.
Royal 8vo, in wrapper, - - - 0 1 0
———— Cloth, - - - - 0 1 6

The Pupil's Hand-Book, being the Exercises contained in
the foregoing Work. For the use of Classes and Schools. 2 Parts,
sold separately—each - - - - 0 0 3

MUSIC—*Continued.*

A Junior Course of Instruction in Singing on the Letter
Note Method. Arranged progressively on the same plan as the
Graduated Course, and specially for the use of Schools and Junior
Classes. Nos. 1 and 2 published—each £0 0 1

An Elementary Course of Practise in Vocal Music, with
numerous Tables, Diagrams, etc., and copious Examples of all the
usual Times, Keys, and Changes of Keys. For use in connection
with any method of Solmization. By David Colville. Complete
in 2 Parts—each 0 0 4

Colville's Choral School; A Collection of Easy Part Songs,
Anthems, etc., in Vocal Score, for the use of Schools and Singing
Classes. Arranged progressively, and forming a complete Course
of Practice in Vocal Music. In 20 Parts—each ... 0 0 4

Choral Harmony, in Vocal Score, for the use of Choral
Societies, Classes, Schools, etc. Edited by David Colville. 100
Nos. published. List on page 13. Royal 8vo—each - ... 0 0 1
———— Nos. 1 to 16, in Illuminated wrapper, stiffened, - 0 1 0
———— Nos. 17 to 34, in Illuminated wrapper, stiffened, - 0 1 0
———— Nos. 35 to 50, in Illuminated wrapper, stiffened, - 0 1 0
———— Vol. I. (50 Nos.), cloth boards, - - 0 4 0
———— Vol. II. (50 Nos.), cloth boards, - - 0 4 0

Naismith (Robert). The Story of the Kirk.
A Sketch of Scottish Church History for Young Persons. Super royal
32mo, cloth extra, gilt edges, - - - - 0 1 6

Ned Fairlie and his Rich Uncle. And other Tales.
Super royal 32mo, cloth, Illustrated, - - 0 0 6

Newlyn House, the Home of the Davenports.
By E. A. W. Extra fcap. 8vo, cloth, with Illustrations. - 0 2 6
———— Extra cloth, gilt edges, - - - 0 3 0

Newton (John). Cardiphonia; or, The Utterance of the Heart.
Extra fcap. 8vo, cloth, - - - - 0 3 0

Nothing to Do; or, The Influence of a Life.
By M. H., Editor of "The Children's Hour." Royal 32mo, cloth,
Illustrated, - - - - 0 1 0

Ocean Lays; or, the Sea, the Ship, and the Sailor.
A Selection of Poetry. By the Rev. J. Longmuir, LL.D. Royal 16mo,
cloth, Illustrated, - - - - 0 2 6

Patterson (Alexander S., D.D.) The Redeemer and the Redemption.
A Series of Sacramental Discourses. Extra fcap. 8vo, cloth, - 0 2 6

Red Velvet Bible (The Story of a).
By M. H., Editor of "The Children's Hour." Royal 32mo, cloth,
Illustrated, - - - - 0 1 0

Rosa Lindesay, the Light of Kilmain.
By M. H., Editor of "The Children's Hour." Extra fcap. 8vo,
with Illustrations, - - - - 0 2 6
———— Cloth extra, gilt edges, - - 0 3 0

Sangreal (The); or, The Hidden Treasure.

By M. H., Editor of "The Children's Hour." Super royal 32mo, cloth, bevelled boards, Illustrated, - - - £0 1 0

Short Stories to Explain Bible Texts.

By M. H., Editor of "The Children's Hour." With Illustrations.

1. Minnie and Letty.
2. Willie Lewis and his Schoolfellows.
3. Discontented Susy.
4. Charlie Grant and his Sister Nina.
5. Ned Fairlie and his Rich Uncle.
6. Annie Ross; the Little Housekeeper.
7. Little Jephy; the Adopted Child.

8. Harry Westbrook's Visit to Grandpapa.
9. Mr Granville's Journey.
10. Stella Howard and her Morning Calls.
11. Bertie and Ethel; or, Self-Denial.
12. Little Milly and her Half-Crown.

Done up in a neat Illuminated Packet, 32mo, - - £0 1 0
In cloth extra, gilt edges, - - - - - 0 1 6

Short Tales to Explain Homely Proverbs; a Series of Reward Books.

By M. H., Editor of "The Children's Hour." With Illustrations by Charles A. Doyle.

1. Who Gives Quickly Gives Twice.
2. Short Accounts make Long Friends.
3. Evil Communications Corrupt Good Manners.
4. Forgive and Forget.
5. Handsome Is who Handsome Does.
6. Better Late than Never.

7. Do as You Would be Done by.
8. A Stitch in Time saves Nine.
9. Where there's a Will there's a Way.
10. All is not Gold that Glitters.
11. Waste not, Want not.
12. There is no Place like Home.

Done up in a neat Illuminated Packet, 32mo, - - £0 1 0
In cloth extra, gilt edges, - - - - 0 1 6

Stars of Earth; or, Wild Flowers of the Months.

By Leigh Page. With upwards of 50 original Illustrations by the Author. Crown 8vo, cloth extra, gilt edges, - - - 0 5 0

Steele (James). A Manual of the Evidences of Christianity.

Chiefly intended for Young Persons. 18mo, cloth, - - 0 1 0

Stocking Knitter's Manual (The).

A Companion for the Work Table. By Mrs George Cupples. Extra fcap. 8vo, Illuminated Cover, - - - - 0 0 6

Story of Daniel (The).

From the Original of the late Professor Gaussen. By the Author of "The World's Birthday." Extra fcap. 8vo, cloth, with Illustrations,
(In Preparation.)

Sunday School Photographs.

By the Rev. Alfred Taylor, Bristol, Pennsylvania. With Introduction by John S. Hart, LL.D., Philadelphia, U.S. Extra fcap. 8vo, cloth, printed on toned paper, - - - - 0 2 6
—— Extra cloth, gilt edges, - - - 0 3 0

Tales for the Children's Hour. By M. M. C.

Royal 32mo, cloth, Illustrated, - - - 0 1 0

Thomson (Rev. Andrew, D.D.) Sketches of Scripture Characters.

Crown 8vo, cloth extra, gilt edges, with Illustrations, - - 0 5 0

Thomson (Rev. John.) The Domestic Circle; or, The Relations,

Responsibilities, and Duties of Home Life. Extra fcap. 8vo, cloth, 0 2 6
—— Extra cloth, gilt edges, - - - - 0 3 0

Thoughts on Intercessory Prayer. By a Lady.
Royal 32mo, limp cloth, - - - - - £0 0 6

Turnip Lantern (The). And other Tales.
Super royal 32mo, cloth, Illustrated, - - - 0 0 6

Two Friends (The). And other Tales.
Super royal 32mo, cloth, Illustrated, - - 0 0 6

Tytler (C. E. Fraser). The Seals and Roll of St John.
Demy 8vo, cloth, - - - - - 0 7 6

———— **The Structure of Prophecy and of the Apocalypse.**
Demy 8vo, cloth, - - - - - 0 3 6

———— **The Apocalypse.**
Demy 8vo, cloth, - - - - - 0 5 0

Wallace (Rev. J. A.) Attitudes and Aspects of the Divine Redeemer.
Extra fcap. 8vo, cloth, printed on toned paper, - - 0 2 6

———— **Pastoral Recollections. Third Series. 1853—63.**
Extra fcap. 8vo, cloth, printed on toned paper, - - 0 2 6

———— **A Pastor's Legacy. Being Brief Extracts from the MSS.**
of the late Rev. A. B. Nichol, Galashiels. With Introductory
Notice. Extra fcap. 8vo, cloth, printed on toned paper, - 0 2 6

———— **Communion Services According to the Presbyterian Form.**
Extra fcap. 8vo, cloth, printed on toned paper, - - 0 2 6

———— **Waymarks for the Guiding of Little Feet.**
Extra fcap. 8vo, cloth, printed on toned paper, - - 0 2 6
———————— Extra cloth, gilt edges, - - - 0 3 0

Wallace (Rev. J. A.) James Nisbet. A Study for Young Men.
Extra fcap. 8vo, cloth, printed on toned paper, - - 0 2 6
———— Extra cloth, gilt edges, - - - 0 3 0

Watts (Isaac, D.D.) Divine Songs for Children; with Scripture
Proofs. For the use of Families and Schools. Square 32mo, sewed, 0 0 2

White Roe of Glenmere (The).
By Mona B. Bickerstaffe. And other Tales. Extra fcap. 8vo, with
Illustrations, cloth, gilt edges, - - - 0 3 0

Wilberforce (William). A Practical View of Christianity.
New and Complete Edition. Extra fcap. 8vo, cloth, - 0 2 6

Wise Sayings, and Stories to Explain them.
By M. H., Editor of "The Children's Hour." With Illustrations

1. Jamie Wilson's Adventures.	7. The Nutting Party.
2. Little Silphy.	8. Castles in the Air.
3. The May Garland.	9. The Turnip Lantern.
4. The Visit to Eden Park.	10. The Lost Brooch.
5. The Two Friends.	11. The Village Favourite.
6. Alick Watson and his Quaker Friend.	12. The Gold Medal.

Done up in a neat Illuminated Packet. Super royal 32mo, 0 1 0
In cloth extra, gilt edges, - - - - 0 1 6

Witless Willie, the Idiot Boy.
By the Author of "Mary Matheson," etc. Royal 32mo, cloth,
bevelled boards, Illustrated, - - - - 0 1 0

CHORAL HARMONY,

FOR THE USE OF CHORAL SOCIETIES, SCHOOLS, ETC.

Price One Penny each Number.

Those numbers marked † contain easy Music for Elementary or School practice.
Those marked * have an Accompaniment.

SACRED.

3. O praise the Lord. - - - - - - - Colville.
6. Pray for the peace of Jerusalem.
   Hark, the loud triumphant strains. (*12th Mass.*) - - - Mozart.
†7. Brightest and best of the sons of the Morning. 3 *v.* - - Webbe.
   The Lord is my Shepherd. - - - - - - Pleyel.
   Be joyful in God. - - - - - - - Colville.
   Characters used in Music.
†8. Musical Signs and Abbreviations.
   How firm a foundation. - - - - - Mozart.
   From Greenland's icy mountains. - - - - - Banister.
†11. To us a Child of hope is born. - - - - - Mason.
   Hark, the herald angels. - - - - - Arnold.
   Hallelujah. - - - - - - - R. A. Smith.
14. Make a joyful noise. - - - - - - R. A. Smith.
   Sanctus. - - - - - - - - Camidge.
15. Sing unto God. - - - - - - - R. A. Smith.
17. Great God of Hosts! - - - - - - Fowlie.
   O God, forasmuch. - - - - - - Fowlie.
*20. Blessed is he that considereth the poor. - - - - R. A. Smith.
22. Hymn on Gratitude. - - - - - - Holloway.
*24. Come unto Me.
   Now to Him who can uphold us. - - - - R. A. Smith.
26. O Father, whose almighty power (*Judas*). - - - Handel.
*28. There is a land of pure delight. - - - - Colville.
*31 & 32. The earth is the Lord's. - - - - - R. A. Smith.
*35. Jerusalem, my glorious home. - - - - - Mason.
*38. Hear those soothing sounds ascending, - - - - Beethoven.
*39. Walk about Zión. - - - - - - Bradbury.
   He shall come down like rain. - - - - - Portogallo.
*43. Blessed are those servants. - - - - - J. J. S. Bird.
   Enter not into judgment. - - - - - J. J. S. Bird.
*47. Ode on resignation. - - - - - - Colville.
†48. Hark, the Vesper Hymn. - - - - - Russian.
   The hour of prayer. - - - - - - Douland.
   Thanksgiving Anthem.
   God save the Queen.
†50. God bless our native land.

CHORAL HARMONY—*Continued.*

	Forgive, blest shade.	*Callcott.*
	Morning Prayer.	*Herold.*
51.	We come, in bright array (*Judas*).	*Handel.*
	Lead on, Lead on (*Judas*).	*Handel.*
†54.	Ye gates, lift up your heads.	*Dr Thomson.*
	O send Thy light forth and Thy truth,	*R. A. Smith.*
†56.	Who is a patriot.	
	Praise the Lord.	
	Gently, Lord, O gently lead us.	*Spanish.*
	Joy to the world.	
†59.	With songs and honours.	*Haydn.*
	Hymn of thanksgiving.	*Mason.*
	God is near thee.	
60.	But in the last days.	*Mason.*
*64.	Great is the Lord.	*American.*
	Arise, O Lord.	*American.*
*69.	Awake, awake, put on thy strength, O Zion!	
*70.	I will bless the Lord at all times.	*R. A. Smith.*
*71.	Hallelujah! The Lord God omnipotent reigneth.	*R. A. Smith.*
	God, the omnipotent.	*Russian National Melody.*
†72.	The brave man.	*H. G. Nageli.*
	Lift up, O earth!	*G. F. Root.*
	From all that dwell below the skies.	
	When shall we meet again.	
	O wake, and let your songs resound.	*Himmel.*
	All hail the power of Jesus' name.	
*75.	Blessed be the Lord.	*R. A. Smith.*
	Great and marvellous.	*R. A. Smith.*
*77.	Grant, we beseech Thee.	*Callcott.*
	Come unto Me when shadows darkly gather.	
79.	The Lord is my Shepherd.	*Beethoven.*
	Let Songs of endless praise.	*Mason.*
	My Faith looks up to Thee.	*Mason.*
81.	Beyond the glittering starry sky.	*J. Husband.*
82.	Blest Jesus, gracious Saviour.	*Michael Haydn.*
	Hymn of Eve.	*Dr Arne.*
	Salvation to our God.	
84.	I will arise.	*Richard Cecil.*
	Blessed are the people.	
86.	I was glad when they said unto me.	*Dr Callcott.*
87.	Hark! above us on the mountain.	*C. Kreutzer.*
88.	Then round about the starry throne.	*Handel.*
*91.	Oh! how beautiful thy garments, O Zion.	*J. A. Naumann.*
*92.	Put on thy strength, O Zion.	*J. A. Naumann.*
*98.	Sing to the Lord, our King and Maker.	*Haydn.*

The Series to be continued

CHORAL HARMONY—*Continued.*

SECULAR.

1. Let no dark'ning cloud annoy.	- • • • -	*German.*
The Reapers. -	• • • -	*Colville.*
2. There is a Ladye sweet and kind. -	• • • -	*Ford.*
Gentle Spring.	• • • -	*Colville.*
4. And now we say to all, Good-night. -	• • • -	*Methfessel.*
The fountain. -	• • • -	*Colville.*
5. Good Morning. - • -	• • -	*Bradbury.*
Swiftly, swiftly, glide we along. -	• • • -	*Colville.*
†9. May-Day. *Colville.*—Harvest time.	• • -	*Storace.*
Glossary of musical terms.		
†10. Spring-time. *Silcher.*—Freedom.	- • -	*Scottish.*
Rosy May. *Scottish.*—The Daisies.	• • -	*Mozart.*
†12. Summer's Call. • -	• • -	*Colville.*
Midnight.	• • -	*Donizetti.*
13. Hark, the Curfew's solemn sound. 3 v.	• -	*Attwood.*
16. Serene and mild. -	• • -	*Webbe.*
18. How sweet, how fresh this vernal day.	• -	*Paxton.*
Stars of the summer night. -	• • -	*Cokking.*
19. Thyrsis, when he left me. -	• • -	*Callcott.*
21. The Coquette. The Exquisite. -	• • -	*Neithardt.*
Aldiborontiphoscophornio. 3 v. -	• • -	*Callcott.*
23. Swiftly from the mountain's brow. -	• • -	*Webbe.*
*25. It is better to laugh than be sighing.	• • ' -	*Donizetti.*
27. Hark, the hollow wood surrounding.	• • -	*J. S. Smith.*
It was an English Ladye bright. -	• • -	*Hine.*
†29. Joyful be. *Schneider.*—Sweet peace.	• • -	*K. Smith.*
O lady fair. The last rose of summer.	• • -	*Moore.*
30. The Skylark's song. - • -	• • -	*Mendelssohn.*
Spring Morning.	• • -	*Schneider.*
†33. Come and join our trusty circle.	• • -	*Gabler.*
The Forest. *Karew.*—Sweet love loves May.	- • -	*Silcher.*
*34. Glad May-day. - • • • -	• -	*Neithardt.*
36. Good-night. - • -	• • -	*Hulme.*
Bright, bubbling fountain. -	• • -	*Waelrent.*
37. From Oberon, in fairyland. -	• • -	*Stevens.*
*38. The Chapel. - • -	• • -	*Kreutzer.*
†40. 'Tis dawn, the Lark is singing. -	• -	*G. Webb.*
Thrice hail, happy day. -	• • -	*German.*
Home! Home! - • -	• • -	*Pax.*
Come joy, with merry roundelay. -	• • -	*German.*
41. Sweet Echo, sweetest nymph. -	• • -	*Birch.*
*42. The Gleaners. -	• • -	*Mendelssohn.*
*44. The Sight Singers. - • •	•. • -	*Martini.*
Hail, festal day. -	• • -	*Rossini.*
45. Thy voice, O Harmony. -	• • -	*Webbe.*
46. Rural pleasure. - •	• • -	*Kreutzer.*

CHORAL HARMONY—_Continued._

See the Sun's first gleam.	*Schuffer,*
49. The Sprite Queen.	
The Sun's gay beam.	*Weber.*
Behold the morning gleaming.	*Weber.*
52 & 53. All the Choruses usually performed in Locke's Music for Macbeth.	
55. Hail, smiling morn.	*Spofforth.*
See our oars with feather'd spray.	*Stevenson.*
57. Come, gentle Spring.	*Haydn.*
†58. Never forget the dear ones. 3 v.	*Root.*
Merrily o'er the waves we go.	*Bradbury.*
The foot Traveller.	*Abt.*
61. The Chough and Crow. 3 v.	*Bishop.*
62. The huge globe has enough to do. 3 v.	*Bishop.*
63. May Morning.	*Flotow.*
Come to the woody dell.	*Pelton.*
65. Which is the properest day to sing?	*Arne.*
Beat high, ye hearts.	*Kreutzer.*
66. Now strike the strings.	*Rudd.*
Since first I saw your face.	*Ford.*
67. Step together.	- *Irish Melody.*
For Freedom, Honour, and Native Land.	*Werner.*
The Mountaineer.	*Tyrolese Melody.*
What delight, what joy rebounds.	*German.*
68. Come, let us all a Maying go.	- *L. Atterbury.*
Hark, the Lark.	- *Dr Cooke.*
Here in cool grot.	*Lord Mornington.*
*73. Come on the light winged gale. 3 or 4 v.	*Callcott.*
*74. Sleep, gentle Lady.	*Bishop.*
76. Sparkling little fountain.	*Bradbury.*
The dazzling air.	*Evans.*
*78. On Christmas Eve the bells were rung. 3 or 4 v.	*P. King.*
80. Hail, all hail, thou merry Month of May.	*G. Shinn.*
83. The sea, the sea, the open sea.	*C. S. Neukomm.*
85. The Singers.	- *C. Kreutzer.*
89. Call John.	*American.*
The Travellers.	- *James King.*
90. Laughing Chorus.	- *G. F. Root.*
Soldier's Love.	*E. Kucken.*
*93. Foresters sound the cheerful horn.	*Sir H. R. Bishop.*
*94. Gaily launch and lightly row.	- *Mercadante.*
My lady is as fair as fine.	- *John Bennett.*
*95. See the bright, the rosy morning.	- *Carl Blum.*
The land of the true and brave.	- *Franz Abt.*
*96. What shall he have that killed the deer?	*Sir H. R. Bishop.*
*97. The Song of the New Year.	*Donizetti.*
*99. Why should a sigh escape us?	*Otto.*
How sweet the joy.	- *C. Kreutzer.*
*100. Upon the Poplar bough.	*Paxton.*
Mountain Home.	- *C. Kreutzer.*
Over the Summer sea.	*Verdi*